BAFFLED BY LOVE

Stories of the Lasting Impact

of Childhood Trauma

Inflicted by Loved Ones

LAURIE KAHN

SHE WRITES PRESS

Published 2017
Printed in the United States of America
Print ISBN: 978-1-63152-226-0
E-ISBN: 978-1-63152-227-7
Library of Congress Control Number: 2016963209

For information, address:
She Writes Press
1563 Solano Ave #546
Berkeley, CA 94707

Cover design © Julie Metz, Ltd./metzdesign.com
Interior design by Tabitha Lahr

She Writes Press is a division of SparkPoint Studio, LLC.

To Natalie Haimowitz, PhD, who taught me about love.

CONTENTS

PART 2

PART 3

Prologue

Martha points to the potted ivy plant with brittle leaves drooping on my window ledge. "For God's sake, Laurie," she says. "What kind of therapist has plants that are half dead? You're going to scare your clients off. You really should water them."

Martha is tall. Her hair is tucked under a Yankees baseball cap; although she now lives in the Midwest, we both understand that, in her heart, she is a New Yorker. Martha's edginess and honesty are part of the intimacy we have developed. She is a truth-teller. There have been times that others (her family and strangers on the street) have wished she was softer and less confrontational.

I have told Martha, "You cannot get out of your car at stop signs and yell 'motherfucker' at the annoying driver in front of you, behind you, or next to you. The drivers may be crazy or dangerous. They can hurt you." On other occasions, I have said, "Martha, it is a bad idea to rage at your husband, and an even worse idea to do it in front of your children."

I have learned over many years that Martha's combative behavior and brutal honesty cover depths of grief and pain from too many losses suffered too young, from too much heartbreak with too little comfort.

In ten years of therapy, Martha has come far. She has learned to trust me and allows me to be her companion in dark places. She has shared with me the pain she suffered when she was twelve years old and her beloved adoptive mother died, leaving her in the neglectful custody of her father and stepmother. She has wept and faced the piercing grief of her brother's suicide with me, and spoken of the horror of being raped by her babysitter in her bedroom while her father and stepmother, steeped in alcohol, remained oblivious downstairs.

Martha is fierce, courageous, and resilient. I saw her rally after she found her birth parents and met the four sisters they chose to raise. After years of hiding in her bedroom, high on drugs and ashamed, Martha has gotten sober and made amends to her own children for the pain she caused them while she was abusing drugs. She no longer—well, less frequently—yells obscenities at her husband, and she never yells at him in front of the children.

Today, as our session comes to an end, Martha gets up and saunters toward the door of my office. She rests her hand on the doorknob, turns back to look at me, and says, "I love you."

I smile warmly—but behind my warm smile, I am in a mild panic. I think to myself, *Caring? Sure. Compassion? Definitely. Fondness? Absolutely. But love? Is that going too far? Wouldn't that push the limits of the sacred client-therapist relationship, with its clear, well-defined boundaries?*

I worry that I could be walking into dangerous terrain, the dreaded emotional quicksand that can derail even the best therapy. Tragic stories of therapists sexually exploiting their clients haunt us and fill the annals of our profession. We are trained to respect boundaries, to convey respect and provide consistency and predictability—these, we are told, are the foundations of good therapy. I sit in the black chair with the padded arms, and my clients sit in either the purple tweed chair or the tan cloth chair for their fifty-minute sessions. It's all very orderly and predictable. Predictable is good. A colleague once said he thought he bored his clients into health.

In the lives of my clients, Martha included, the people who were supposed to love and protect them instead trampled the boundaries of their body and spirit. In their lives, love went terribly wrong.

I've spent hours pondering the complexities of love. I have written articles for professional journals about the traumatic experience of love created by child abuse; I have taught many therapists about the treatment of relational traumas. Yet in this moment with Martha, I am confused and speechless.

She reaches the end of the hallway. She turns around to look back at me one more time and says, "You know, it wouldn't kill you to say you loved me, too."

She awaits my response.

Introduction: **THINKING ABOUT LOVE**

When they were children, my clients were abused by someone they believed to be trustworthy—someone who professed to love them. Their wounds are often invisible to an untrained eye. And they blend in. They are social workers, teachers, lawyers. They are students, single fathers, at-home mothers who attend yoga classes. They vary by age, class, culture, and sexual orientation.

Love is why they come to therapy. Love is what they want, and love, they report, is not going well.

Early and ongoing abuse harmed my clients' self-esteem, causing symptoms of post-traumatic stress and feelings of undeserved shame that they carry like phantom limbs. What they have in common is damage to their capacity to create intimate and loving relationships.

Their abusers—a father, stepfather, priest, coach, babysitter, aunt, neighbor—are usually people who inhabited their daily lives. Maybe their abuser introduced them to the pleasures of Beethoven and Mozart, or taught them how to ride a bicycle. They offered love when caring was otherwise in short supply.

Kristy's father never missed her swim meets. Betsy loved talking with her father, a beloved college professor, about the works of Dickens, Joyce, and Faulkner. Diana's stepfather faithfully picked her up after school every day. Joe's mother was his anchor after his philandering father walked out on the family. But these very people—the people who should have loved and protected my clients—are the people who abused and frightened them.

Perpetrators groom their young victims, using cycles of trust and betrayal to manipulate and seduce them. Grooming is emotional foreplay; it mimics attunement, caring, and empathy. It distorts love and renders it unrecognizable.

For three decades, I have been treating clients whose understanding of love has been twisted by abuse. I mentor clinicians, arming them with skills and teaching them the painstaking, treacherous, and life-giving art of treating traumatized individuals and their families. Even gifted clinicians quickly discover that what they learned in school does not suffice in practice. As our clients invite us to listen to their untold stories, we become witnesses to crimes that occurred behind closed doors. For both client and therapist, trauma shatters core beliefs and decimates assumptions about the benevolence of the world.

I never dreamt of specializing in trauma. As a young therapist I thought I could learn to spot trauma and refer those clients to someone more skilled and braver than I. But this work has changed me and inspired me in ways I could never have imagined.

This book contains true stories that my clients have shared with me. Stories of their resistance and of their determination to know and understand what has interfered with their desire to love and be loved. Stories of the families in which my clients learned corrupt models of love. Stories of the rugged terrain we have traveled, where toxic love stories have faded and my clients have come to know and recognize a new kind of love.

When I began this book, I did not intend it to include any of my own story. I was proud and confident, and felt compelled to write about what I had learned from my experience as trauma therapist, teacher, and mentor. With my clients, too, I rarely share details about my life or about my past. I am a rather private person. So I am a little mortified by the amount of memoir that has slipped into this book. At first these scenes were just part of the process—an accident of sorts, something to help me get to the "real stuff," my work with clients. Memoir was not a direction I wished to explore. Yet over time I came to realize that intertwining my own stories with my clients' was more honest and human. Could I match my clients' bravery and share my own stories about love gone wrong?

I have never claimed to be an expert in love. In fact, I have failed in matters of love almost as often as I have succeeded. Like many of my clients, I did not grow up with good models to emulate. The truth is, between the client and the therapist is our shared humanity, flawed and glistening.

So I took a dash of courage from my clients. I included scenes from my childhood and stories about my perplexing adolescence, where love became more suspect. I shivered when I found myself writing about my first marriage, in which beliefs formed in my childhood reappeared. I wrote about how and where I truly learned about a better kind of love. Strands from my story and from my clients' stories are interwoven throughout, whispering back and forth.

At times, we are all baffled by love.

—Laurie Kahn, 2016

PART 1

*"Love that excludes honesty does not
deserve the name of love."*
—Alice Miller, *The Body Never Lies*

Chapter 1: DON'T LIKE ME

The water cooler in the waiting room looks like a plant stand with an upside-down bottle on the top. The walls in my waiting room are painted dusty blue, which the painter promised would be soothing. Kristy is the first and only person here. Her eyes are glued to a *National Geographic* magazine.

"Hi. You must be Kristy."

She looks up, nods, and follows me into my office.

Kristy perches on the edge of the brown tweed couch that rests against the wall and folds her hands neatly in her lap. From this vantage point, she can see everything in the room: the framed photos of children's faces from my trip to South Africa, the plants on the windowsill, clay statues of two women smiling and laughing, the papers scattered over my desk.

"What brings you here?" I ask.

"The social worker I met told me that you are the go-to therapist around here if you had a crappy childhood."

Kristy wears no jewelry or makeup. Her unstyled hair and rimless glasses suggest she has mastered the art of staying as invisible as possible.

She burrows deeper into the couch and looks past me to the three large windows. Outside, the branches of an oak tree stretch past the second-floor office window. The leaves are bright orange and yellow. The impatient autumn arrived early. Chicago is temporarily aglow before the swift arrival of winter.

"Two weeks ago, everything fell apart," Kristy says, describing the morning she unraveled. "I awoke to a mountain of my kids' laundry. Different sizes of inside-out blue jeans, my boys' white underwear mixed with Ginger's colored underpants, T-shirts dripping with dirt and sweat and mounds of unmatched socks. My bed felt like quicksand. After staring at the pile of kids' clothes, I turned over and went back to sleep. I was sinking into a very dark place. I didn't care if I ever woke up."

Kristy momentarily glances up to the fan on the ceiling. "I don't know how long I was asleep. When I opened my eyes, my Saint Bernard was standing over me with his slobbery mouth in my face. He licked my cheek and then my ear. He knew I had to get up and take care of my children. I crawled out of bed, but I could not face the laundry or my crying children. I called a friend to watch my kids. In a haze, I drove myself to the hospital."

I say, "Some part of you knew exactly what you needed to do." Kristy is resourceful; even in the throes of her despair, she mobilized to get the help she needed.

"I guess so. When I got to the hospital, some shrink doctor asked me questions and then promptly admitted me to the psych ward. I'm ashamed to say this, but I loved being in the hospital."

"What did you like about being there?"

"I liked the people in the hospital. They were real, honest. No one hid anything. When I'm with the moms in my neighborhood, I feel different, more broken."

I scribble the words "no one hid anything" in my notepad.

"We had groups every day after breakfast where we learned skills for handling things. Each group session had a topic, like how to identify emotions. They taught us that we could have feelings and not act on them. It's this thing they called 'mindfulness' or 'compassionate noticing.' They talked about how to soothe ourselves when we got overwhelmed or upset. I still have a binder with all the lessons. They gave us handouts with exercises to practice. I hope I can join a group here, too. Oh, yeah, and I had art therapy sessions in the afternoon, which was great." She pauses. "It's funny. I have an advanced degree, even if it is just in fine art. You might think I would know how to do these simple things, but I don't."

"It's great you were able to learn those skills," I say.

"Well, 'learned' might be an exaggeration, but it was a start. I want to be able to teach these things to my kids."

"How old are your children?"

"Three, five, and seven."

"That's a big job." I empathize with the strain of taking care of three young children.

Kristy's shoulders droop. "When my three-year-old cries, I want to yell, 'What the hell do you want?' For days, sometimes, my kids get something resembling a sandwich for lunch and dinner. I don't think they know what a hot meal looks like. My Saint Bernard knows more than I do about being a good mother. He is always patient and loving." She looks down at the floor. "I want my children to feel safe and loved." She flicks a tear from her cheek. "I really just want to be a good mother."

Then her tone brightens. "So, I was wondering," she says, "if you might have a manual or something I can read that will teach me how to do that?"

I smile. If it were that easy, I would gladly give her one. I gently probe to learn a little about her childhood. "Kristy, how would you describe your parents?"

She is sitting on her hands, like a child trying to not touch forbidden objects. "My sister and I used to say that we were the only children remaining in our family; we used to joke that the others didn't make it."

A chill moves down my spine. I have developed a finely tuned ear for clues of childhoods where things went terribly wrong. I am used to snippets that hint at untold stories. "Can you tell me why it was a challenge to survive in your family?"

"I never really understood why other people looked to their parents for support," she says. "I thought you were doing well if they just didn't sabotage you, like trip you on your way out the door." She looks to the side. "My mother wasn't cruel. She just wasn't. She was clueless."

"Ouch," I say softly. "What about your father?"

"My father was crazy and abusive."

I am struck by the economy of her words, and the weight of them. "Is there anything else you want me to know about your father?"

"No, I hate talking about him. I have to get better," she says. "I owe it to my children."

Having children frequently leads people to enter therapy. They may have buried memories of their turbulent childhoods for years—and then, without warning, moments with their own children hurl them back into the painful feelings and memories of their past. Sometimes this happens when their children turn the age they were when their abuse began. Like Kristy, they realize that they have to do something, heal something, to ensure that their children will experience a better childhood than their own.

For Kristy, parenting is like hiking in the wilderness without a map, without the knowledge that she'll need food and water to sustain her or a flashlight for when night falls. No one ever told her or showed her the ways of the world, the basics. For Kristy, normal has always been a guessing game.

I look at the large black clock on the wall and see we are almost out of time. I ask if there is anything else she would like me to know.

Kristy's brown eyes fix on me. "I want to be very clear about something: I do not want you to like me. I do not want you to care about me." For the first time, I hear intensity, an urgency. She takes a deep breath. "I just want you to help me."

For Kristy, allowing someone—allowing me—to care about her would be like choosing to play in traffic with a truck heading right toward her. She fears reliving what she learned during her childhood, when those who should have cared for her injured her instead. The damage, the soul-crushing damage, of such betrayal is that relationships, tenderness, and empathy are no longer a source of soothing. The child becomes vigilant, on guard, watching to see which parent is home: the nice one, or the one that scares them or hurts them?

Kristy fears that care and love are indelibly linked with betrayal.

I will later learn that when Kristy was a child, before she knew the word or the meaning of sex, her father began sneaking into her room at night. Unlike many other clients I have seen, Kristy has no ambivalence about her father. She hates him and can't remember feeling otherwise.

Her mother, meanwhile, behaved as though food and shelter were all that children needed. She turned a deaf ear to what happened in Kristy's bedroom across the hall. Indeed, both her parents, whose job was to love and protect her, failed to do so.

Don't care about me, Kristy cautions me. *Don't like me.* She asks if we can simply bypass the essential ingredients of attachment and emotional safety.

I do not say that this is impossible. I want to thank her for warning me to tread cautiously. I need to respect her well-earned trepidation about closeness and deep connections; these feelings take her to the burning ashes of her childhood, the place where things went terribly wrong.

Kristy presents a great therapeutic challenge—both for her and for me. If we can weather the storms to come, she can have a reparative experience where my care for her and my delight in her will allow her to heal. But for her, therapy itself is a source of fear, not comfort. She will need to learn to tolerate our relationship for her therapy to be successful. I will need to be tolerant of her resistance to closeness and soothing. The relational traumas of her past will vibrate between us.

Kristy makes an appointment for the next week. As she gets up to leave, she says, "I would never have walked in here if it wasn't for my children."

Chapter 2: **A NICE VISIT**

I wait on a corner in Baltimore, scanning the cabs, searching for my mother's silhouette. At the age of ninety, she has taken a train from New York and then a cab to my hotel so that she can share a weekend and some meals with me, her youngest daughter.

A cab stops in front of me. My mother emerges. Her freshly applied red lipstick matches her grey and red paisley scarf. She squints in the fierce midday sun, her gold-plated clip-on earrings glistening.

"Oh darling," she says, "I am so glad to see you."

"How was your trip?" I ask.

"Oh, wonderful. A very nice man helped carry my suitcase down the stairs."

My mother's arms reach to pull me close for a hug. I coax my body to relax. To not stiffen. I want this last chapter of her life, of our relationship, to go well. The wounds from my childhood have faded. We are good friends now.

Later that afternoon, we take a bus to the Baltimore Museum of Art. Betsy (I always call her Betsy; it suits her better than Mom) loves art and museums.

We climb the twenty steps to the entrance side by side.

"Careful. Watch your step," I say, gently taking her arm to steady her.

Moments later, panting slightly, we enter the museum. We admire *Purple Robe and Anemones*, the famous Henri Matisse painting of flowers that is reproduced on posters and T-shirts and sprawled on umbrellas. Up close, the purple, red, and white flowers look like they are dancing in their purple vase. One of the few things Betsy and I both enjoy is vases filled with flowers.

We stroll, my mother and I, through the exhibits, sometimes arm in arm. "Don't touch," the signs warn. Works of art are placed precisely for the eye to embrace. Everything is neatly framed; there are no messes. Betsy is at home here. She is delighted, as she always is when surrounded by beauty.

Later, we take a water taxi to Fell's Point. The moon, my mother notes, is waxing or waning—she forgets which is which, but no matter. We are together; the lights of the cityscape are behind us and in front of us. What could be nicer?

In a nearby restaurant, I request a quiet corner so Betsy's loss of hearing won't impede our conversation. We each have a glass of white wine. This is delightful; everything is going well. My mother tells me she loves me and adds that she is proud of me. What more could a daughter want?

"You are so good with people now," she says. "I am so happy to see you warm up so well to them."

I want to say to her, "Yes, I am no longer the surly, withdrawn ten-year-old who tortured you. You know, the one that refused to be charming to impress your friends." But I refrain. I also don't say, "Being good with people is how I make a living." But no matter. She is ninety, and we are having a nice visit.

We return to our hotel. Betsy is excited to give me the necklace she has brought for my birthday. It is wrapped in turquoise tissue paper with a purple bow that curls at the edges. I unwrap it, and she places the necklace around my neck and carefully closes the clasp. "This looks nice against greens, blues, and black, really with anything," she says. My mother has an eye for style and for real gems.

The next day, we have lunch at a restaurant overlooking the harbor. My mother has agreed that I can ask her a few questions—questions I have wondered about for many years. Being a writer has allowed me at times to pose undercover in my own family.

"So, Betsy, do you mind if I start with when Susan and I were little?"

"Oh no, dear, I don't mind."

"When my sister and I were babies, you spent very little time with us. You've said you didn't like to hold us or feed us a bottle. Why was that?"

"I think I felt inadequate. Mostly it was that I was afraid of babies."

I hope I will discover something—an insight, a revelation, even a small peek into my mother's psyche.

"I was afraid I might drop the baby," she says.

So that is the great phobia that gave you a pass on mothering your children? I think to myself. *Who isn't afraid of dropping a baby?*

"The nanny took care of you and Susan. Pedro, the handyman, helped me out on the nanny's day off. I was so anxious on Thursdays, when the nanny was gone." Then she adds, "I did like to visit you children."

Visit? I write the word on my napkin. Over the years, I have collected many scraps of paper with words or comments of my mother's that have momentarily startled me. I think to myself, *You visit animals at a zoo, not your own children in the nursery*, but I say nothing.

"I don't mind if you take notes," Betsy says agreeably.

I pause to catch my breath.

"I have some questions about your relationships with men." Since my early teens I have been privy to mother's world of lovers.

"Go ahead. I don't mind at all."

"How long did your first affair last?"

"Well, if you mean with Joe, that was my second affair. My first one," she says unabashedly, "was when your father was in the army. I was so lonely. But if you mean Joe, ten years, I think. Joe was handsome and he was very successful. He wore me on his arm like a trophy." She seems to be enjoying the conversation.

"Did you ever think about divorcing my father?"

"No, never. We had fun, we had good friends, and we went to lots of parties together. Your father was the life of a party and we had two children."

Betsy picks up her spoon to sip the warm clam chowder she ordered. "Fish is always a good idea if you're eating at a restaurant on the water," she says.

My salmon and dill quiche sits untouched on the china plate. "Were you ever in love with my father?"

"I don't know. Honestly, I am not sure if I have ever loved anyone. I am not sure I know how to love."

Not anyone? I am speechless. I have no more questions.

The waiter brings the check and places it on the table. I take out my credit card to pay for lunch.

"Thank you, darling," she says.

As we get up to leave she adds, "Let me know if you have any other questions."

⸺

The next morning, I am irritable. Fragments from the conversations with my mother play like background noise—just loud enough to bother me, but not loud enough to fully grasp.

It has been a good visit; I mean, we are being kind to each other.

After a quick cup of coffee, we check out of our hotel and I take her to the station. I carry her bag down the steep stairs. We wait together in silence. Then the tunnel is filled with the roar of the train as it approaches track six and stops in front of us.

I hand my mother her black carry-on suitcase. She kisses me on the cheek. I wince just a tad.

She climbs up two steps and boards. I wave good-bye.

The train pulls out of the station and accelerates down the tracks, the wheels clicking and clacking against the rails. As the train recedes into the distance, taking my mother with it, I feel a flush of emotion. I am startled by a sudden urge to run beside the train, to find my mother's compartment, to see her face once more. I want to yell, "Hey, lady! I was that little girl that you came to visit from time to time!"

Chapter 3: SHARING STORIES

Ten minutes before Group begins, I create a circle of seats. Two brown tweed couches face each other: one in front of the window, the other against the deep purple wall. A South African tapestry hangs above the second couch; its woven threads are a tribute to a community determined to heal. It is a small token from my trip to Cape Town in 1996, where I witnessed Nelson Mandela and Bishop Desmond Tutu initiate the hearings of the Truth and Reconciliation Commission. The tapestry is an inspiration, my secret prayer shawl.

I flick the wall switch off and leave a lamp aglow in each corner of the room. The members of Group do not like the harshness of the overhead lights. I place throw pillows on the couches and find the plush purple blanket—the one Wendy likes to wrap around her shoulders—and put it on the right side of the couch where she always sits. I move several chairs between the couches and add three small wooden tables to hold a variety of to-go cups filled with coffee, Diet Coke, and herbal teas. I water the ivy plant on my windowsill with the remains from a cup left by an earlier client. The brittle corners of the leaves beg for water.

Group is where I am most alert. For thirty years, I have led these sessions for survivors of childhood trauma. Group is complicated and sometimes uncomfortable, but I trust the power of communities to heal. Group creates something bigger than and complementary to individual therapy. On good nights, it is where my clients find their voices and share common experiences. Shame is replaced with pride and self-respect. Group experience contrasts with the impoverished relational and emotional environments its members have previously known. In a sense, it is a training ground for healthy and intimate relationships.

I, too, feel less isolated in Group. Although the language of therapeutic relationship embraces empowerment and mutuality, I feel that wisdom and health are disproportionately attributed to the therapist, and woundedness and need to the client, in this field. Our clients' gifts are often underutilized and underacknowledged in one-on-one sessions. In Group, however, everyone is both a recipient and a provider of insights, wisdom, and compassion.

I am fond of this community of women who bare their souls, share their stories, and are compassionate witnesses to each other's struggles and triumphs. Many of them have been coming here for years; this is their emotional home. They know how to talk about betrayals and abuse; they are determined to make changes to improve their lives. They are willing to confront the ways in which their histories of abuse and neglect intrude on their present relationships. For others, the two hours is an endurance test filled with anxiety and apprehension. Those who are mothers, like Kristy, are determined to break the legacies of abuse they've inherited and give their children the care and protection they deserve.

I place my lukewarm cup of herbal tea on the small table next to my black padded chair. The smell of cinnamon wafts upward. At precisely seven o'clock, I open the heavy, solid wood door and each woman enters and finds her place. Most of them sit in the same spot every time, as if they have assigned seats.

Kristy arrives on time after feeding her three children dinner. She sits on the beige chair near the door where she can keep one eye on the exit. Wendy sinks contentedly into the right corner of the couch in front of the wall and places her super-size Diet Coke on the small side table. Jessica sits facing the window on the left side of the couch. Erin, a newer Group member, quietly walks over to the tan chair across from me, next to Wendy. Diana is often late and takes whatever seat is vacant.

This is Meg's first night in Group. She takes the chair next to me.

Kristy always brings something to knit, bead, or weave. Using her hands helps her tolerate the intensity of the conversations. She is eager to connect with others, but she is also easily spooked. Sudden movements or unexpected gestures of warmth frighten her. What is most disconcerting to her is that she can't yet connect the dots; she is mystified by her own reactions. She is learning to manage them, however, and to express to others what she is experiencing. It may seem odd to think of participating in therapy as requiring skill, but it does. Kristy is learning how to tolerate strong feelings without collapsing or dissociating.

She is also learning how to soothe herself in the face of her anxiety. Tonight, her calming strategy requires yellow, green, red, brown, white, and black blocks of clay, which she offers to share with everybody in Group.

Diana is skeptical of Group. Given her past, there is no reason for her to trust the others or me. I think it is a small miracle that every Wednesday night the morsel of hope she still has allows her to walk through the door.

I may be pushing my luck, but tonight I ask Diana if she would like to go first. "Is there something that you want to work on tonight?" I ask.

"Work on," in the language of group therapy, translates to: Is there something you want to change about yourself that is interfering with creating the life you desire?

"Okay, I guess. I can go," Diana says reluctantly. She finds talking about herself unfamiliar and uncomfortable. "I had kind of a crappy week."

I lean in to hear her. When she talks about herself her voice is soft and lacks inflection.

"My boyfriend is really bugging me. He sits on the couch, watches TV, smokes pot, and never helps around the house. When we first met, he was a lot of fun. His daily pot smoking didn't really bother me. Now, he won't get his fat ass off the couch. If I was dripping blood on the floor, he wouldn't notice." Diana's boyfriend's behavior echoes the indifference of her childhood caregivers.

"Have you told him what you want or need from him?" Jessica asks.

"What's the use? He doesn't give a shit."

"How do you know he wouldn't care if you don't try?" Jessica suggests.

"He leaves his crap all over the house. I hate living in a mess," Diana says, ignoring the suggestion. She appears cold, angry, and unforgiving. Her anger turns her face to stone. "Sometimes I think I would be happier living alone, but I can't afford the rent by myself."

Kristy shares with Diana that for years she had big fights with her husband about cleaning the house. "It took time, but he is getting the hang of it. Things really did change."

Diana is unmoved by Kristy's encouragement. Her disappointment with her boyfriend fits her like a pair of comfy old jeans. She distrusts those who profess to care about her.

As a child, Diana had no one to comfort her. She did not speak to anyone about her stepfather's nighttime visits. She mastered dissociation, disconnecting from her body to escape her pain and fear. She survived years of abuse by checking out to avoid feeling overwhelmed by her distress.

Perhaps she needs Group to feel her hopelessness instead of trying to make her feel better. Yet I have a strong desire to win her over from the dark side, to show her that warmth and caring can be part of the landscape she inhabits.

In Group there is sometimes a powerful undertow. Members feel a pull to reenact relationships formed during their traumatic

pasts—and subconsciously, others in Group are invited to participate, to take a place in a drama with perpetrators, victims, rescu-
ers, and bystanders. If the people in Group continue to try to help
Diana and she continues to dismiss and reject what they offer, they
will become annoyed. I do not want Diana to recreate with us the
rejection that is familiar to her. I want to help her have a different
outcome, however small.

"Diana, I notice what people are saying to you does not seem
to be helping. Do have any idea how we can be helpful?" I ask.

"No, not really."

"I have a feeling you are used to having to handle things on
your own."

"That's for sure," she affirms without hesitation.

"I wonder if you would be willing to tell us something
about you that we don't know. It doesn't have to be earthshak-
ing, just something."

"I have a dog named Queeny," she says with surprising
enthusiasm. The volume of her voice increases several decibels; I
no longer have to strain to hear her. "Queeny is part Border Collie and part something else. I found her at a shelter two months
ago. We go on long walks in the woods."

"Your face lights up when you talk about her," I observe.

"She is amazing. She is really beautiful."

"Would you bring a picture of Queeny to Group next week
so we could see this beautiful creature?"

"Yeah, I can do that."

"That would be cool," Kristy chimes in. "I love dogs. I can't
imagine my life without my Saint Bernard, Grindel."

Diana and Kristy share a fleeting smile, a flash of connection.

I scan the faces. I see others are now looking at Diana with
less frustration as she shares her affection for her dog. Out of the
corner of my eye, I see that Kristy has quietly placed on the side
table by Diana a miniature white rabbit with red ears that she has
just made of clay.

This is good, I think to myself. I turn my attention to Meg, our newest member. She looks frozen. She is tall, awkward. Her size thirteen shoes seem cumbersome. Though she is in her forties, I imagine her towering over boys when she was in grade school, her shoulders stooped, hoping no one would notice this body she unhappily inhabits. She has not said a word yet.

Jessica looks at Meg and asks, "What brings you to Group?"

Meg blurts, "When I was eight, my brother sexually abused me. I think the sexual abuse stopped at eleven, but only because he went on to my next sister. He got three of us, skipping the two in the middle. He was violent and crazy. He beat us, too."

Jessica looks stunned.

Meg speeds ahead; she does not pause or notice others' reactions. "My dad would say, 'Leave the girls alone.' He smacked my brother around and beat him pretty good, but then my parents would go out and leave us alone with him. Once, my brother tried to strangle my sister. I got a baseball bat and hit him on the back."

Meg's story is spilling out. She is not narrating her story; she is vomiting the details. I watch the other members' eyes shift from warm and welcoming to glazed. Their bodies begin to recoil, and they look away from her.

"Meg." I say her name firmly to disrupt her monologue. "You have shared a lot." I say it compassionately, but she looks past me and cannot respond. I want to encourage her to slow down, to breathe. I want her to occupy her body and to feel what she is narrating. She is unaware of what she is feeling, let alone what the impact of what she is saying is having on the others.

Meg has no brakes, no dimmer switch, just two settings: shut down or full-throttle ahead. These are the polarities of post-traumatic stress. When Meg switches to "on," she becomes anxious and dysregulated. She is flooded with feelings that overwhelm her capacity to integrate or manage the story she is telling. When she switches to "off," she is isolated, and her trauma goes underground.

I ask Meg if she would be interested to hear what others are experiencing as they listen to her. I think this will be good for her, and I am also aware that the others need to recover from the inundation of details they've received from this person who has just come into their treasured space.

"Yeah," Meg says. "That would be good."

The others rise to the challenge. One tells Meg she knows it can be hard to come to Group; she recalls how frightened she was on her first night. Another congratulates Meg for beginning. Several acknowledge that they had a hard time listening as Meg talked graphically about her childhood.

These women in Group are not neophytes. They have grace as they speak about the things that were once unspoken. They are generous; although not always pleased to welcome a new person to Group, they are willing to share what they have gone through and what they have learned. Their lives are better than they once were; indeed, their lives are a testament to hope. Their ability to empathize, to tell the truth, to be of use to each other is the blessing of Group.

Trauma is hard to speak about and hard to hear about. But stories unshared don't disappear; they return in relationships, silently taking prisoners. If the trauma remains unknown, unspoken, and unconscious, it does harm. Telling your story to a compassionate witness, in contrast, can be healing.

In Judith Herman's seminal book *Trauma and Recovery* (1992), she warns us that the most common mistake in trauma treatment is avoiding the traumatic material altogether while the second most common mistake is going toward the traumatic material too soon without the establishment of a therapeutic alliance.

The now accepted standard of care for the treatment of trauma is a phase-oriented approach. The first phase is about safety and stabilization; it's about building a therapeutic alliance and developing skills for tolerating and identifying feelings. Meg is describing what happened to her, but she does not know how to allow us to be a source of comfort. She is heading into the traumatic parts of her childhood too quickly, sharing with a group of people who are still strangers rather than companions who have earned her trust.

"Meg, can you tell us what is going on in your life right now that you hope you can change by being in Group?" I ask.

"I am afraid all the time for my son. I can't let him use a public bathroom. My son says to me, 'Mom, that's nuts. I have to use the bathroom.' So I let him when I have to, but then I stand guard outside the bathroom like an idiot."

"How old is your son?" I ask.

"Eight," she says.

"He is the age you said your abuse began."

Meg relaxes; her gangly body melts into the chair. Her eyes focus on the women in Group as if she is noticing them for the first time.

Erin is sitting on the edge of her chair, fidgeting with her shirt. "Could I go next?" she asks. She looks wholesome, squeaky clean; her freshly washed hair gently frames her face. She is in her late twenties, several years younger than the others in Group.

"Sure."

"This weekend I was with my family and, as usual, there was tons of tension between me and my mom. I don't want to cut off contact with her, but I hate who I become when I am around her. I am enraged. I feel like such a brat."

Erin's speech is hurried. I speak slowly in response. "Erin." I hold her gaze. "Could you say more about what was stressful about your visit with your mom?"

"My mother is very mean. She is mean to me and to my siblings. It's like she has license to hurt us whenever she wants. She has been emotionally scarring to me and to everyone in my family."

An interesting word, "scarring." Her mother has inflicted wounds that left marks that never fully disappeared.

"My mother," Erin adds, "is manic-depressive."

I wonder how Erin has been affected by her mother's illness. She has shared with me that her mother is very volatile, and that her illness is currently untreated. Part of the time her mother isolates in her bedroom; other times she is verbally abusive. Like others in Group, Erin lacked the safety and reassurance of a stable and loving home as a child.

"I guess the good thing is it made me independent," she says after a pause. "I know how to do things. I learned to rely on myself." She states this with an air of pride.

Diana nods. She recognizes that independence can be the unfortunate consolation prize of neglect.

"Do you get along with the other people in your family?" Wendy asks.

"I am very close with my dad," Erin says. "I've talked with my dad a lot about how upset I am with my mom."

"That's cool you have someone to talk to." This is the first time Diana has spontaneously responded to anyone in Group.

"This weekend, my dad suggested that I get together with him and with my mother so I can confront her about her constant verbal abuse," Erin says.

I believe in accountability, and I often encourage open communication with family members—but in Erin's case I am concerned. Both Erin and her father agree that her mother is okay about 5 percent of the time. To me, those are not betting odds.

"Erin, from what you've shared about your mom and about her illness, it seems unlikely that talking to her about the abuse and sharing your feelings with her will have a good outcome. I wonder if your father minimizes the extent of your mother's untreated illness and the devastating impact it has on you and the rest of the family."

Erin quickly comes to her father's defense. "My dad lives with a steady diet of verbal abuse from my mom. I get to leave and go back to my apartment; he is stuck with her."

I gently ask her if she ever wishes her father had been more protective of her and her siblings.

"I am very close to my dad," she repeats, this time more emphatically. "I have always been able to talk to him about anything that is bothering me. I don't understand why he puts up with my mom. Maybe he thinks it is just what he has to do to be a good person."

It does not occur to her that her father is not just another family member who is equally victimized by the erratic and disturbing behavior of her mom. He is her father, and he is responsible for the welfare of his children. It does not occur to her that both of her parents have responsibility for the impact they have on the children they love.

"Erin, I wonder if it is frightening to think about being mad at your dad."

"Yes," she says. She is silent for a few long seconds then says, "He is all I have."

The clarity of her statement about her dad moves me. Her relationship with him is both precious and fragile. Erin cannot yet afford to see her father's flaws. It is too risky. With an ill mother, he is and has been her only lifeline.

It is nine o'clock. Group is over. Members collect their purses, backpacks, and sweaters. Kristy, Diana, Jessica, Wendy, and Erin converse with each other. Meg stares at her feet and walks quickly out the door. They all file out of my office, down the long hallway, and into the night.

I close the door, take a deep breath, and exhale. I am exhilarated and exhausted. I am in awe of the power, generosity, and courage of these women.

I turn to my desk to straighten up a bit before I go home. I notice something new on my desk: a small brown dog with yellow eyes, made out of clay.

Chapter 4: QUILLS OF A PORCUPINE

When Wendy comes for her first appointment, she acts more like someone dropping in on a neighbor than a client meeting a therapist.

She plunks down on my couch. Her round body sinks into the tweed cushion. She runs her fingers through her curly red hair. "So," she asks, "Where do you want to start?"

"Well, how about you start with what brings you here?"

"Okay, if you really want me to." She places a large Diet Coke on the table next to her. "I suck at relationships. I'm thirty years old. I want to have a family some day. I have no clue how I can get from here to there."

"Can you say more about how you suck at relationships?"

"Mostly I hide out in my apartment. Once in a while, I force myself to go out with the other nurses after work. I visit my family on some weekends, but being with them always depresses me. Oh, and men terrify me."

I am fascinated by the way what might initially appear to be neurotic, disturbed, or even pathological behavior makes sense as a way of coping with traumatic experiences. I imagine Wendy's current avoidance of relationships is a clue to injuries she endured in the past.

"Wendy, that's a lot. Let's take one at a time. Start with your friendships." I prefer to start on the outer edges, furthest from what I suspect are the more traumatic injuries.

"In the beginning, things go well. There's just some point when something inside of me clicks and I just don't ever want to see them again, so I stop answering the phone when they call."

"Did something in your past friendships become burdensome or ungratifying?" I ask, seeking her interpretation of what goes wrong.

"I wouldn't put it that way. It's just that I am always the listener; no one ever asks how I am doing."

"I bet that gets old," I say.

"No, I wouldn't say that. I just lose interest."

"You mentioned that your family was depressing," I say, moving in one layer.

"Yeah, there is so much chaos. Their house is filled with stuff—so much stuff that I can barely move from one room to another. It makes me crazy. When I go visit them, there isn't a chair I can sit on without moving piles of junk."

"Was your home like that when you were growing up?"

"Well, when I was a kid, instead of stuff there were kids everywhere. Sometimes there were as many as ten foster kids plus my other siblings."

"Oh my!" I say clumsily. "What was that like, to grow up with so many kids around?"

"It was okay. I took care of the little ones. I think I was changing diapers and cooking dinner by age five, maybe younger. I can't remember a time when I wasn't taking care of them."

"Would you say that you became a kind of surrogate mom for those children?"

"No, not really. I just did what had to be done. I cleaned the house, took care of the babies, did the dishes, and got good grades. The other kids were always in some kind of trouble or fighting."

"It seems like you had to be the good child."

Wendy shakes her head. "No, I wouldn't say that."

"You had a great deal of responsibility, taking care of others at a very young age. Do you think that was costly to you in any way?"

"Not really."

I realize that I sound detached, more clinical than human. I want to understand Wendy and the world she inhabited, but I am struggling to make a small connection with her; she is deflecting my every attempt. Her round face, soft red curls, and sparkling blue eyes invite connection, but her hard-wired distrust is like the quills of a porcupine.

I try a more open-ended question. "Is there anything else about your family you think might be important for me to know?"

Wendy tells me she was one of her mother's five children. Three were adopted, but she was born to her mother—a fact at odds with her feeling of not belonging. Of all the kids, she is the only one who successfully finished college and now holds a steady job.

"At any time," Wendy explains, "there were up to fifteen kids living in my house. Sometimes a social worker would come to our house and we would turn the trundle beds into couches and hide some of the children because we were over the limit of foster kids that were allowed."

I am captivated by her stories. My mind wanders to the many stories I have read of gentiles hiding Jewish children in their attics, in their cellars, or behind a farmhouse in their barn—but I am not sure if the children in Wendy's story were being protected or harmed by those efforts to hide them.

"Were you close to any of the kids?

"Some of them. Two of them are dead." Wendy shares this startling detail nonchalantly.

"Dead?"

"My brother, the dead one, was messed up on drugs. He came to our house with a knife one time, looking for me. We didn't allow weapons in the house, so I stopped having any contact with him. My other brother sexually abused me, but I don't think he knew what he was doing." Her tone is flat, as if this is an unimportant detail.

I try to imagine the house where Wendy grew up. She calls it "chaotic." Was it a sanctuary for children in need of a home and loving family, or something more sinister? I can't tell, but my curiosity has begun to yield to my sense of alarm. I confess to Wendy that I am fascinated and also a little horrified by what she's told me.

"Really? Horrified? That's weird."

This is the first of many moments in which Wendy is baffled by my responses. "I never brought friends home," she continues. "There were so many crazy things going on. I was told that what goes on in the family must stay in the family."

Wendy tells me story after story, like a skilled immersion journalist. She is privy to this chaotic family, yet she has an uncanny detachment from it. I realize she is disobeying the no-talk rule demanded by her parents, so I ask her, "How is it for you to tell me about your family?"

She reflects only briefly before saying, "Okay."

I glance at the clock and am surprised to see our time is coming to an end. "Is there anything else you think I should know today?"

"No, not really."

Wendy is bright, but she is unable to reflect on the meaning or impact of what she knows. Her defenses are well earned and intact. Her parents gave refuge to neglected and abandoned children, but they didn't provide the safety those children or she needed. She was harmed by this chaotic family. Her brother sexually abused her; too much was asked of her at too young an age. She does not consider anything that happened egregiously out of line, just thinks her story is a bit out of the ordinary. She minimizes the significance of these experiences and their impact on her life. Yet she recognizes that her relationships aren't working, and she'd had the courage to come for help.

A day later, I receive a message from Wendy:

"One of my hopes in working with you and your expertise is to gain not only a sense of safety, but also a sense of sexuality and a normalcy in relationships. I'm not sure if I've truly loved anyone, not sure what love looks like or what love feels like. I've been to college, have a job that I enjoy, I own a car and home, and I have my health. But sometimes I wonder if I wouldn't give it all up to have a healthy relationship."

Wendy wants to learn about love. I am surprised and impressed that she is so forthcoming, articulate, and unflinching about expressing her yearnings.

Today, Wendy calls before our scheduled appointment and cheerfully informs me that she has decided not to come in. It appears we are playing hide-and-seek. As a child, if she hid in the midst of the chaos, I'm sure she was left hiding indefinitely.

"Wendy, it's your choice," I say. "You get to decide if you come. I would really like to see you. If there is something difficult about coming here today, we could talk about it together."

"Why does it matter if I come?" she says. "You hardly know me. The way I see it, if I were to get hit by a bus tomorrow and die, it wouldn't matter."

Wendy has a tremendous ability to care for others in need. She works with sick and disabled children. But she is not able to see others, including me, as a source of care or comfort. It is going to be difficult to earn her trust.

I imagine the two of us in a boxing ring. The bell chimes. We fight many rounds. If all goes well, there are no knockout punches. We are both determined, sometimes exhausted. We struggle, but I believe it will, in the end, be entirely worth it.

Reluctantly, Wendy agrees to show up for her appointment. When she arrives, she sinks back into my couch, her arms folded across her chest. This time, she appears defiant. Her blue eyes still sparkle but her quills are at the ready.

"Okay, here I am," she says. "What now?"

"How you are doing?"

"Crappy," she says.

"Could you tell me a little more?"

"What is talking about it going to accomplish?"

Wendy reminds me of the kids I knew when I worked in group homes who wore distrust like a badge of honor. They dared me to care about them. This kind of dare appeals to me. I remember the secret pride I felt as a child when I hid my pain and loneliness from others. A tough exterior covers a trove of hidden longings. Allowing someone to care can expose festering wounds.

"Wendy, I don't know if it will do any good to talk about what's bothering you, but as long as you have to pay me for today, you might as well give it a try."

Wendy laughs. "So ask me something," she says defiantly—but also, I suspect, with a tinge of hope. Because she has no idea how to have a relationship in which her needs, fears, or desires are the focus, she needs me to initiate connection. This is a familiar pattern for people whose parents were preoccupied, depressed, or traumatized, and who deprived their children of comfort and safety. I have only just begun to know Wendy, but the damage the absence of an early, secure attachment did to her is painfully evident.

"Tell me about one of the children you cared for who lived in your family's house," I say.

"Timmy," she says quickly. "He was a special needs kind of kid. I worried about him; he was really sweet. Every day, I checked on him after school. I created games we could play together. He didn't get much attention."

"Why not?"

"I guess everyone was busy. I remember how bad the basement room smelled from his urine-soaked bed sheets."

"Wendy, that sounds awful."

"He couldn't walk on his own, so I took him outside in a red wagon. He giggled so hard when the wheels of the wagon crackled over the railroad tracks. Back and forth over the tracks we went. It was his—our—favorite activity."

"You look so tender when you talk about him." I am moved by her ability to love and care for Timmy.

Wendy continues as if I haven't spoken. "One day, when I came home from high school, I went down to his room in the basement to see him. He looked grey. I told my mom, 'Timmy doesn't look right. He needs help.' She ignored me. I carried him in my arms and put him in my car. I drove him to the emergency room."

My hand is over my mouth. "My God, Wendy, that's awful. You must have been so frightened."

"Yeah, I guess. The doctor said he was dehydrated and very sick."

She is telling me a story about neglect; a story about a mother who knew little about caring for children yet had fifteen of them in her care. She is also giving me a glimpse into what I imagine is a sea of unexpressed grief. A sadness wells up in my throat, but Wendy's face is impassive. I feel the grief that she can't yet afford to feel.

"Did he get better?"

"No. He died in the hospital the next day."

"Oh my God. That's heartbreaking." My words are inadequate. I am appalled by the situation and in awe of this heroic child. I hope the expression on my face will help Wendy realize the magnitude of what she endured and of what she has had the courage to share.

Wendy tells me more stories I will later learn she has never told before. "When I was nine years old, my older brother—you know, the one who sexually abused me—pushed me down the stairs and I broke my arm."

"What did your parents do?"

"Oh, I didn't tell them what happened. We never tattled on each other. In some ways, we protected each other. I also figured if I told my parents, they wouldn't do much to stop it and they would blame me for what happened. And if my brother found out I told them, he would beat the crap out of me."

Wendy's narrative does not acknowledge the daily abuse and neglect she endured as a child. I want her to learn a different kind of loyalty—loyalty that is earned and does not allow secrets when you are injured, violated, or abused.

Secrets are a curse for abused children. But Wendy couldn't risk telling her mother or anyone else; she knew she would not be believed. When a child dares to tell someone about their abuse and they are disbelieved, it is even more devastating. The child is more vulnerable to shame, less willing to turn to others for support and soothing in times of distress. The symptoms of post-traumatic stress are more pervasive. We speak of this as the "trauma after the trauma." For Wendy, it was like playing double jeopardy, with all the odds stacked against her.

"What horrible choices," I say. "You had nowhere to turn."

Wendy glances at the ceiling. Her arms are relaxed; her hands gently rest on her thighs. She can't acknowledge her parents' gross lack of responsibility or the severity of the crimes she witnessed. She is not ready to grieve the loss of all losses when love fails.

The time has evaporated; I tell Wendy it is time for us to stop.

"Really?" she asks. "It seems like we just started."

"How was being here today?" I ask.

"A little better. You know, I hate shrinky stuff. I like it better when you are just real like you were today."

I understand. She wants me to be direct and not give her what she calls therapist-like responses. She appreciates when I express my feelings and share what I am thinking rather than hiding behind neutral-sounding questions.

"That's a deal," I say. "Real is good."

Wendy rises from the couch. "I'll see you next week," she says confidently.

Chapter 5: LOVE OUTSOURCED

It's not that I was unloved as a child. It's just that in my family, those things were outsourced. My sister and I believed our collie, Bali, was our surrogate mother. We learned to walk by grabbing her tail for balance. When I was in grade school, Bali walked me across the football field, past the six swings, and across the dirt baseball diamond to the metal fence. Bali waited on the sidewalk as the crossing guard waved his hand to signal that I could cross the street to Greenacres School.

When school was out, I went back across the grassy football field and whistled, and Bali came running, wagging her tail, to escort me home. She was joyful and dependable, and although I could run faster than many of the boys in my class, Bali always won when we raced to the birch tree that marked where the baseball field melted into my backyard.

Collies can do many things, but they fall short when it comes to cooking breakfast or cutting the crust off your peanut butter and jelly sandwiches. So Lizzie, with her Irish brogue, came to live with us when I was two. "Live with us" seems cozier than to say she was hired by my parents to take care of the children. She traveled by boat from Ireland to New York at the age of nineteen. But as luck would have it, she needed me as much as I needed her.

When Lizzie arrived, I moved out of the bedroom I shared with my sister, Susan, and into Lizzie's bedroom. Lizzie's bedroom was smaller and simpler. It did not have any of the girly things in my sister's room: the flowered wallpaper, the pink-and-yellow bedspread and matching curtains, the painted shelves filled with our stuffed animals, the thick yellow carpet that bounced back after I ran on it in my bare feet.

I slept in a twin bed separated from Lizzie's by a white metal table. White window shades kept out the light in the mornings. A woven throw rug with shades of blue lay in front of the white metal dresser, covering the cold spot on the floor. Our room was simple and perfect.

My favorite part of each day was bedtime. Lizzie would lather a cream on her hands that smelled like the roses in our backyard; then she'd sit on my bed and tuck me in. I would say the prayer she taught me: "Now I lay me down to sleep. I pray the Lord my soul to keep. If I should die before I wake, I pray the Lord my soul to take. God bless Mommy, Daddy, Susie, and, of course, Bali and Lizzie." This was a strange ritual for a Jewish girl, but it was our special time together. Lizzie would kiss me and whisper, "Good night, little darling," and I would drift into sleep.

My parents said that Lizzie was part of the family. My father joked with her, teased her about her cooking and about her boyfriends who came to the house—clear signs of his affection.

When I was four and my sister, Susan, was six, our cousin Mary got married, and we were invited to the wedding. My mother left our dressy clothes neatly on the bed. Lizzie's task was to dress my sister and me in our matching yellow dresses and black patent-leather shoes. She told us we would be flower girls at the wedding. Susan and I would walk side by side down the grassy path behind Mary, holding flowers.

"Maybe someday you will be brides," she added.

"Ick." I winced. The yellow dress was enough to bear. I was a girl whose fantasies were not of fairy princesses dressed in fancy gowns. I preferred my cowboy outfit: brown pants with fringes down the sides, and a wide-brimmed hat with a cord under the chin that fit perfectly on my head.

Lizzie laughed and continued to gently brush my hair. She tied white silk sashes around our waists as if we were Christmas presents. My sister twisted and turned, enjoying a Shirley Temple moment. I felt miserable all dressed up like a doll.

My mother came to check on us, aglow in her fancy clothes. "Oh, you girls look beautiful," she said.

My father proudly drove our new red DeSoto with power steering and power windows to my aunt and uncle's New Jersey country estate. My mother stretched out in the large passenger seat. Lizzie sat squished between Susan and me in the backseat. After several hours, pebbles crackled under the tires as we cruised up the long driveway. The sun was bright; the apple trees seemed to be magically refraining from dropping their apples on the well-manicured grass. The sky was clear blue with a blush of feathery white clouds in the distance, perfect for a fairy tale wedding.

When the ceremony began, my parents were seated together under the apple tree. Susan and I walked through the archway glazed with red roses. I squeezed the bunch of white and red tea roses in my small hand, stepping nervously behind the train of my cousin's flowing white gown. I was afraid I would step on her delicate dress and ruin everything. I searched the crowd for Lizzie's face. She waved at me, and I relaxed.

After the I-do's, Mary rushed over to the rose bushes to toss the bouquet. It floated for a moment above the sea of giddy, eager women. Lizzie leapt for the bouquet and caught it.

My aunt and my grandmother were furious; my mother was embarrassed. The hired help had caught the blessed bouquet. My sister and I jumped up and down with excitement, unaware of everyone else's dismay.

Many mornings, the policemen from our town could be found sitting around our kitchen table. They had Irish accents, just like Lizzie. She offered them hot coffee. Chatter and laughter warmed the kitchen. "Good morning, little one," a handsome policeman in his freshly pressed blue uniform would greet me as I ate my oatmeal. I knew they liked Lizzie. I think they liked me, too.

Their affection for us became evident during a big winter snowfall when Bali, who wandered freely and knew every corner of the neighborhood, disappeared. Frantically, we searched everywhere for her, but she was nowhere to be found.

The police officers suspended their other duties to scour the area for her. An hour later, a squad car, siren blaring, pulled into our driveway with Bali shivering in the backseat. When she saw me, Bali leapt out of the car, her tail wagging, and ran to me. I kissed her again and again. I didn't mind the taste of her wet fur in my mouth. Tears of relief soaked my face. Lizzie hugged me tight, kissed me, and sent me off to school.

When Lizzie was twenty-four and I was six, she fell in love with Bud, the chief of police's brother. Bud asked my father for permission to marry her. They wanted to start a family of their own. My father gave them his blessing.

Their wedding took place on a hot summer day in a Catholic church with high ceilings. My sister and I were flower girls again.

I don't remember what I wore; I don't remember who helped me get dressed. My father escorted Lizzie in her white gown down the aisle. My sister and I followed behind her until we reached the front of the church, where the priest stood waiting. I sat on a hard wood bench next to my mother. After Lizzie said her vows, Bud raised her veil. I could see her smiling, but she did not see me.

When Lizzie left our house to begin a new life with Bud, I felt a deep emptiness—one that nobody understood. To others, my family was still intact. But I sank into a depression.

Mrs. Jacobs, my second-grade teacher, called my mother to tell her that I had become withdrawn and stopped playing with the other children. My parents were alarmed and promptly sent me to see the school psychologist. This was my first exposure to the world of inkblots and large men who asked children stupid questions. I did not like these men. They would ask me to complete sentences. "My mother_____." I responded, "My mother wears shoes." I worked hard to reveal as little as possible. I was determined that this stranger would not enter my private world of sorrow and emptiness.

If I had lost my mother, no one would have wondered why I was depressed. If my mother had died, I could have joined a group for kids who had also lost their moms. We could have shared our grief and buffered each other from feeling different from the other kids who still had moms. Maybe Mrs. Godin, our next-door neighbor, would have invited me over for homemade cookies after school. She might not have known how to talk to a grieving six-year-old, but she could have stared at me sympathetically as I ate her chocolate chip cookies, leaving traces of chocolate on my face. If I had lost my mother, the teacher would have been informed that I had suffered a horrible loss. She would have paid special attention to me during this troubled time.

These things did not happen, and my distress remained a mystery. I did not know what was wrong with me; I did not know why I was so angry or why I had random fits of crying. I did not know why I felt like an outsider in the cheerful world of the other second graders. I did not understand the loneliness that became my frequent companion.

My mother was supposed to be the person who offered me comfort and love, but she was not. My mother was a stylish woman, small-boned and attractive. Lizzie had big hands that could hold a child; her shoulders were broad, her lap was available for me. When I gazed into her eyes, she gazed back. With her, I knew what it felt like to be loved, to have someone whose gentleness calms you before sleep.

My mother's touch was not soothing.

Chapter 6: A TERRIBLE MISTAKE

I return to work after a two-week vacation, feeling relaxed and refreshed. Kristy walks into my office and sits on the brown tweed couch.

I look at her. "I am glad to see you," I say warmly. It is a terrible mistake.

Kristy freezes; her pupils constrict. Wordlessly, she extends her arm rigidly in my direction, breathing rapidly and shallowly. Her hand screams: *Stop!*

I am startled, and so is she. I can see, feel, and almost smell her fear. I have unsuspectingly stepped into an emotional mine field. Beneath us, a ball of terror explodes. I have shown warmth and an interest in her, suggesting caring and connection. Kristy is overcome not with pleasure, as I had hoped, but with fear.

The thing about treating trauma is that behaviors that appear odd, discordant, or startling often have a context, a story. But the context takes time to emerge. In this moment, I need to soothe the woman in front of me, who looks as if she has just been ripped open by a piece of shrapnel.

"Kristy, I am sorry I frightened you," I say calmly. "I can see you are really afraid."

She nods. This is all she can muster. She has no words for what has occurred.

I need to help Kristy awaken from her nightmare to the reality of the day. I ask her to look around the room and describe what she sees. She picks up a heart made of blue glass; her fingers explore the smooth surface. Her pupils and her breathing start returning to normal.

We sit quietly together. She nods her head, signaling to me that she is here with me, shaken but present.

Therapeutic mistakes, like my overly familiar greeting to Kristy that day, can trigger trauma that is beyond words and aches for language.

At the end of the session, Kristy quietly gets up to leave.

"I will see you next week," I say, both as a formality and to reassure her that there is a structure that she can rely on.

She does not look at me but stares at her feet as she walks out of the office.

Our relationship is in its infancy. Her trust—in me, in our work—is fragile. The terror from her past can't be put on hold until our relationship is firmly established. Kristy has shown me that under the surface—neither close enough to be spoken about nor far enough away to hide—is fear and terror. She has shown me that relationships frighten her, and that her sense of safety easily collapses.

The day before her next appointment, Kristy calls me. Her voice is soft and shaky. "I don't want to come tomorrow," she says.

"I really want you to come," I respond. "Would you consider coming and you can decide what we do together? We don't have to talk about anything you aren't comfortable talking about."

"I get to decide what we do?"

"Yep, you decide."

"Okay."

I want Kristy to understand that she has a say in what happens between us. She needs to be confident that her desires and needs will be respected—know that when she feels distress, she can engage with me rather than withdraw.

Kristy shows up for her appointment. She smiles and takes out squares of colored tissue paper from her purse. "I'm going to teach you how to do origami."

I smile too.

Kristy folds the paper, and the edges effortlessly line up. She creates birds and flowers, conjuring art from scraps of paper. I awkwardly and self-consciously fold the thin sheets, attempting to follow her lead. The edges of my bright yellow tissue paper don't meet. Kristy wordlessly guides me. She gently rearranges the papers in my hand so they neatly match. I have to refrain from commenting on what we are doing. Words are my best friends. They soothe me when I am uncomfortable. Kristy, meanwhile, basks in the luxury of shapes and colors; for her, our silence is a relief.

After forty-five minutes, my yellow tissue paper resembles something close to a flower. Kristy's red flower is crisp and finely crafted. She places them both on the table.

"You have placed these two flowers side by side," I say, unable to stifle my desire to verbally make meaning.

"Shhhh." Kristy places her finger gently in front of her lips, signaling me not to say any more. "Laurie, you rely on words too much."

"You are so right," I admit.

Kristy smiles. It is a sweet smile, an innocent smile. "Thanks," she says. "See you next week."

"Thank you, too," I say.

Something is shifting in our relationship. Kristy begins calling me between sessions. I am often sitting at my desk when the phone rings. She has a sixth sense for when I am there.

"Hi," she says. Her voice is soft, young.

"Hey, Kristy," I say warmly.

"I just wanted to hear your voice," she says.

"I am glad you called."

"Okay. Bye."

These short calls move me. Over the next several months, they become more frequent. These lovely flashes of connection are allowing something between us to grow. Call it trust; call it the forming of a therapeutic alliance; call it bonding, attachment, or tenderness—these moments are creating the fertile ground for Kristy to understand love.

———

After a few weeks, Kristy comes in with an agenda: She is worried about her marriage. Her husband drinks heavily, and when he does he becomes loud and unpredictable, which frightens her.

I tell Kristy it is difficult to love someone when you feel frightened.

She nods. "I don't think I can leave him. He supports me and the three kids."

"I am not suggesting that you leave your husband. I wonder if there is a way to talk with him and to find a way for you to feel safer."

"I never thought of that. I figure either you put up with what you have or you leave. This must be that black-and-white thinking they taught us about in the hospital."

"Right. There are more options."

Kristy looks relieved.

"You could begin by talking to your husband about the impact his drinking has on you."

"That's a novel idea," she says.

For Kristy, this is a new concept. For her, relationships have always been something you have to survive. Mutuality—a relationship in which both people's feelings, desires, and well-being matters—is foreign territory.

"You know, my father was a sadistic creep," she tells me. "The more he knew something bothered me, the more he did it. So I never let him have the pleasure of knowing that he hurt me."

Kristy avoids talking about her father. I decide not to probe or ask for any details. Instead I say, "So, talking to your husband and trusting that he would care about your feelings is a big leap of faith."

"That's true." Kristy pauses for a moment. She looks up as if there is a special message written on the ceiling that might help. "My husband is not sadistic. He wants me and the kids to be happy."

During our next meeting, she reports that she spoke to her husband about his drinking. "At first he was really defensive, but I hung in there. I told him that it was really hard for me to talk to him about this. Then he chilled out and he listened. I told him how embarrassed I feel when he drinks and acts goofy and that his mood changes and it scares me. He looked really surprised that I would be scared of him. It was awesome; he agreed that he would try to change. He said that he would just drink a few beers on the weekend."

She grins, looking triumphant. She was able to speak honestly with her husband and feel heard. But she does not linger on the subject of her husband; she returns to the topic that matters to her the most—her children. Kristy beams when she talks about them. She sees each of them as a small wonder endowed with unique gifts and quirks. But she constantly fears that she will fail them.

"My oldest, Eric, had a play date at our house with this nice kid. I am really pleased that he is making friends, but this kid,

Tommy, comes over to play with Eric, and I am so embarrassed because I have a pan soaking in the sink and some of the dishes from last night are not washed."

"You think this small child will be offended by your dirty kitchen?" I ask.

"I know it sounds ridiculous, but I think he will see that I am a neglectful parent."

For Kristy, performing her role as a parent feels like an uphill walk on slippery leaves where she can lose her footing at any moment. She believes she is always one step, one breath away from becoming the neglectful mother she survived as a child.

"What was it like when you were Eric's age and you had a play date?"

"What are you talking about? I didn't even know what a play date was. My mother never would have thought to invite someone over to play with me. I don't think she ever knew the names of any of my friends. Besides, I wouldn't have wanted to bring anyone to my house."

"Kristy, that sounds bleak and lonely."

"Yeah, I guess. I just thought I had to manage on my own."

"You encourage your kids to have friends over even though it makes you nervous. You do right by your children even when you are uncomfortable. That is what a good mother does. Mostly, we are neither perfect nor neglectful moms. We are good enough moms. We all make mistakes. Your mom was not good enough."

Kristy looks relieved.

Chapter 7: TRAUMATIC EXPERIENCES OF LOVE

When victims of childhood sexual abuse are interviewed about their abusers, more than half say they loved, liked, needed, or depended on them. After years of treating and interviewing perpetrators, Anna Salter, one of the great truth-tellers in my field, concluded that "the child's love is both the gatehouse of access and a guard post against disclosure."

Every day after school, Diana's stepfather waited for her in the parking lot. Her mother worked to support the family and was grateful that her husband stayed home. He helped Diana with her homework, and when she joined the track team, he never missed a meet. Diana has no memory of her biological father. Her stepfather was her primary caretaker and her devoted cheerleader. She relied on him.

When Diana was nine, her stepfather began sexually abusing her. He had groomed her until the time was right, and then he took advantage of her trust.

Lily knew little about love. When she was nine, she went to her first sleepover party, and something astonishing happened. After she romped freely with her friend in the back yard; after they got dirty and nobody minded; after they ate dinner with her friend's parents and there was laughter at the table; after all that, something even more remarkable happened. Lily climbed in to the twin bed next to her friend's bed, pulled up the bright green comforter painted with daisies, and watched her friend's mother kiss her daughter goodnight. Then the mom came to Lily's bedside, and with a soft, gentle voice, she said, "Lily." Lily remembers the sweetness when she heard her name. Then the mom kissed her on the forehead and said, "Sleep well."

The next day, Lily was excited to share her discovery with her mother.

"Mom, guess what I learned?" she asked, knowing her mother would never be able to guess. "Parents can kiss their children goodnight."

The sting of her mother's slap doused her excitement.

I ask Lily if she remembers what she felt when her mother slapped her.

"Nothing, I felt nothing. I just never mentioned it again."

For decades people have told me about things that were once unthinkable. Yet I am still stunned when I hear about children like Diana and Lily, who were abused and neglected in their own homes for years and no one—not a mother, not a sibling, not a neighbor—suspected a crime was occurring. At times I think my heart will break when I hear about how a child's yearning for love has been exploited and their innocence destroyed.

I scan the indexes of my twenty-five most read and cherished trauma books, searching for the words "attachment" and "love." There is plenty of discussion of attachment issues, both inside and outside of the therapeutic relationship. But for "love," I find only four references. Some are warnings to therapists about the dangers of love in the therapeutic relationship. James Chu writes," although some caretaking is inevitable and respect is essential, these patients cannot be loved into health." Pearlman and Saakvitne write, "A therapist may explicitly express caring and respect for her client; however, the power and valence of words must be considered. The term 'love' is often sexualized and may imply possessiveness or eroticism."

Is love a secret taboo that is outside the honored discourse of traumatologists, I wonder? Do we see love as something that corrupts, something so potentially dangerous that we dare not mention it? Have we become inured to love after hearing too many accounts of childhoods where loves goes terribly wrong? Have we decided that love is beyond our reach and better left to the poets?

And yet the centrality of love has always appeared relentlessly in my work, like an animal scratching at the door, insisting on being let in.

In 2006, I wrote an article for the *Journal of Trauma Practice* in which I offered a different perspective. "Child abuse, in addition to its pervasive impact on children's development, is a traumatic experience of love," I wrote. This occurs, I continued, "when a child's experience of love, caring, and affection collides with an ongoing experience of abuse and betrayal. The union of love, trust, and safety becomes fractured, while notions of love and betrayal become linked in tragic partnership."

When children are abused by someone who should love them—for Diana, a toxic combination of investment and abuse; for Lily, the absence of love and attention—the result is a traumatic experience of love.

When I first met Diana, the only feeling she expressed was anger with a hearty dash of contempt. Her vulnerability and her longings were securely locked away, hidden from her and from everyone. To this day, her flawless face is devoid of laugh lines, like a porcelain sculpture of a young maiden. She is smart and feisty, and in the rare moments when she lets down her guard, her beauty is almost startling.

One day, Diana mentions the red-and-blue patchwork quilt on her bed that her grandmother made for her. My ears perk up. I wonder, I hope, that maybe her grandmother was a source of tenderness or comfort when Diana was a child. I want to understand what helped sustain her through the years of abuse.

I ask Diana if she can tell me something about her grandmother.

"I can't, really," she says. "I was five when she died." Then she tells me a secret that she has never told anyone before: "I never prayed or anything like that, but at night, the nights when my stepfather was in my bedroom and some nights when he wasn't, I talked to my grandmother. I don't know why I felt so close to her, but I always have. Somehow, I just knew she loved me, that she was listening and that she understood."

"You have found a way to keep her with you," I say.

Many abused children survive on morsels of love. The resilient ones find a kind neighbor, a coach, an imaginary friend, or, as in Diana's case, a beloved grandmother who died several years earlier. When there is even one person they can turn to or confide in, or even the idea of such a person, much is possible.

Diana is able to imagine love; she has the concept of being cherished and understood by someone. And this changes everything. Beneath her impassive exterior is a resilient soul who never gave up on love. This is where hope resides.

Children need to know love. They need someone who is passionately committed to their well-being. Those who know nothing of love, those who cannot imagine love, often lack the capacity to feel empathy and or compassion for others. They are at a greater risk to do harm to themselves and to others.

———

Lily, now in her late forties, is on the verge of leaving her relationship of six years. I ask what she will miss about her partner and the life they built together.

Lily thinks hard about my question. Then she says, "The cat. I will miss the cat. I just couldn't take Brandy because it would devastate my girlfriend."

Lily does not seem to feel conflicted about breaking up with her girlfriend. At first, it is not clear to me why she has come to therapy.

"I know if I leave my girlfriend, she will be really hurt," she tells me. "I feel guilty. I am seeing another woman and she doesn't know about it."

Of course you feel guilty, I think. *You are cheating on your partner.* What I say is, "Do you want to work on your relationship with your partner?"

"No, not really," she replies. "We have a good relationship. We get along well. I just lost interest."

I am struck by how little feeling Lily can muster and how little curiosity she has about the "good relationship" she is apparently about to end.

"I feel nothing about leaving. I wish I felt something other than guilt, but I don't."

"What do you make of this lack of feeling?" I ask.

"I have left other long-term relationships. Maybe it's some kind of pattern. When I left those other relationships, I didn't feel any regret or any sense of loss, either. I just moved on."

Lily's ability to detach, to sever relationships and feel nothing, is a survival strategy that abused and neglected children master to cope with severe hurt and cruelty.

"I feel bad when I hurt people. Even with my aging parents," she adds. "I know I should visit them, but I honestly have no desire to see them. I wish I felt more, but I don't." Lily is numb inside; her feelings are a mystery.

We are both quiet for a long minute, and then Lily looks up. It is the first time her eyes have met mine during this conversation.

"Is there something very wrong with me?" she asks. "I don't think I really know what it feels like to love someone."

What Lily is describing is a serious consequence of early experiences when nurturing and love are absent. Lily has no memories of her mother inquiring about her day, her homework, or her friendships. Her mother showed no pleasure in being her mom. She did not light up when Lily took her first steps or show delight when Lily got the lead in her grade school play. Her father was busy with a demanding career and spent little time with his family. No one in her family ever uttered the words "I love you."

This failure to know love can prove debilitating. Psychiatrist James Gilligan, who worked with death row inmates, expressed this eloquently when he said, "The soul needs love as vitally and urgently as the lungs need oxygen; without it the soul dies, just as the body does without oxygen." Love is the pathway to connections with others; it is the key to our humanity. Love breeds compassion, and it sustains us in the face of adversity. Love creates meaning in our lives. Without empathy or compassion for others, you can harm others and feel little or no regret. Children who are deprived of love have two difficult choices: yearn for love or succumb to numbing indifference and contempt for others.

Lovelessness is excruciating in its banality. It robs a child of her vitality. It leaves no physical welts or scars, just a devastating, enduring emptiness. Lovelessness has no language, poetry, or music. It is unnamed, hidden from view and disabling. Lily, who was deprived of love when she needed it as a child, is now crippled as she attempts to forge loving relationships as an adult. Many assume that the capacity to love is intuitive, but it is not.

Chapter 8: I REALLY LIKE WILLOW

I love training and mentoring therapists. Our work has the power to heal, empower, and change our own lives as well as those of our clients. If we are lucky, mindful, and willing, we too become more fully human in the process.

But this work also has the power to disorient, demoralize, and dishearten the therapists who do it. Do not do this work alone, I caution my mentees.

Today, a new group of postgraduate fellows waits for me with eager faces and notebooks in hand. Anna, Sara, Alissa, Kathleen, and Rachel have come to our counseling center already with advanced degrees, for two years of extensive training in the relational treatment of trauma. They are passionate about this work. They see eight to ten clients and are mentored by a seasoned therapist, and they attend our weekly group and training seminars.

When I began this work in the late 1970s, I was much like them: eager to make a difference, my innocence intact. It was an exciting time. Feminists were fomenting a revolution in the field of psychology. Women met in classrooms and basements and around kitchen tables to question the relevance accepted theories of human development had to women and girls. The prevailing male paradigm placed independence and autonomy at the core; these women argued for the centrality of relationships. It was a new, simple, yet radical construct with vast implications that informed how I would practice as a therapist.

In her 1982 book *In a Different Voice,* Carol Gilligan, PhD, a pioneer in gender studies, revealed that during adolescence, girls are at risk of losing their sense of self-worth and their confidence about speaking up and speaking out. They begin to believe that if they express their true selves, they may be unlovable. But they also feel pressure to engage in love relationships. Songs like "All You Need Is Love," with its innocent and compelling lyrics, support this toxic belief. And in response to these contrary pressures—to be loved, to not lose their authentic selves—girls succumb to unhealthy relationships with themselves and others. This, in turn, places them at risk of depression, eating disorders, and diminished self-esteem. When I read Gilligan's book in the early 1980s, I realized that love, our psychological oxygen, was putting girls and women in great danger.

Something crucial was coming into focus for me back then, and love and connection were at the center of it. Meanwhile, something else was happening that changed me and changed the direction of my work: Women were beginning to speak up about domestic violence, rape, and incest. The numbing silence that had been the norm was replaced by women talking about the abuse they experienced in their homes and on the streets. Until the 1980s, incest especially had been a well-kept national secret. Shame was the great silencer. But then books on incest and sexual assault began emerging. Judith Lewis Herman's *Father-Daughter Incest,* published in 1983, explored the nature of incestuous families. *The Courage to Heal* by Ellen Bass and Laura Davis, published in 1988, provided help for incest survivors. Other books and articles followed, and controversy ensued. Those who spoke and wrote about incest—therapists, researchers and survivors—were accused of lying, exaggerating, or fabricating accounts and memories.

As I learned about recognizing and treating victims of incest, the number of incest cases in my practice multiplied. Had they always been there? Had I not asked the right questions, passively colluding with my clients' denial and our culture's reluctance to admit what happened behind closed doors?

My clients' stories—stories of children who were injured by people they knew and trusted—unnerved me, disoriented me, and eroded my innocence. Not that I was totally innocent: I had grown up with stories about the Holocaust and tragic tales of the lengths to which people would go to protect the people they love. Family, above all, was sacred, and the Nazis took advantage of these bonds to torture their victims. For my clients, this covenant of familial bonds was also destroyed. I wanted to shout at the guests at cocktail parties and at passersby on the streets, "Pay attention! Don't be blind to the everyday abuses occurring around you. Our job is to protect our children, to cherish them!" My world was turned upside down.

Over time, I learned to soothe my own rage and to tolerate listening to my clients' loyalty and fierce attachment to the people who beat them, raped them, or simply failed to parent them. I regained my equilibrium, but I refused to stop being disturbed by the fact that houses full of secrets lined the streets of many neighborhoods—of my neighborhood. I vowed that I would not allow myself to become numb to the devastation caused when love goes terribly wrong, when the very people who are supposed to love and protect you are the ones who hurt you.

This willingness to be disturbed by our clients' stories and to inhabit a world where the balance of good and evil continuously shifts is essential for trauma therapists.

———

The first meeting of the new fellows begins. I ask Rachel if she would like to start by talking about her first meeting with a new client. She gladly agrees.

Rachel is not a novice therapist. She has worked in social service agencies for years, helping clients handle some of life's difficulties. But childhood trauma is outside her experience. She is navigating new terrain.

"Willow is thirty-two," she begins.

Willow. I wonder if she is a child of hippies. Although I am a product of the '60s, I resisted the temptation to name my child Sunshower or Rainbow. I picked Emily Rose. My daughter is grateful for my restraint.

"Willow has six children. Three of them live with her, and three of them live with her ex-husband," Rachel continues.

A large clan, I think to myself, *but hardly an unusual custody arrangement.*

"They got divorced because she left a group she called 'the family,' where they lived and where her husband stayed."

"Odd," I write in the margin of my notebook.

"Willow says she feels empty inside. She is living with a man now whom she describes as nice, a good friend, nothing too exciting. There is a lot she told me, and I don't know what to focus on. I don't want to go too fast with Willow; I want to take time to build trust."

"Rachel, what do you know about this group that she lived with?" I ask.

"She lived there since she was seventeen; her husband is older than her. I am not sure if she picked her husband or if he was picked for her. She said they were not allowed to stay married if they left the group." Rachel reports these facts as if they are quite ordinary.

I wish I were still as innocent as Rachel. I wish I didn't quickly see, smell, and know in my bones that this was going to be a dark story. I proceed cautiously. "It must have taken a lot of courage for Willow to leave this group when the stakes were so high. You might want to find out more about that."

"Okay, that sounds good," Rachel agrees.

The next week, she returns a little less perky than she was last week.

"Here is what I learned," she begins. "Willow's mother was on drugs. When Willow was seventeen, her mother was high and accidentally set their house on fire. The police came, found all sorts of drug paraphernalia, and arrested her mother. Willow escaped and fled town with her boyfriend. At a truck stop, they met some people from 'the family.' She said, 'They were filled with love, and they told me they could see so much beauty in my soul. They promised that they would take care of me. I went with them to their compound.'"

I feel sick inside as I listen to Rachel tell us about Willow. I imagine vultures circling this seventeen-year-old girl who has just lost her home and her mother. Like a pedophile offering a child candy, they offer Willow a family and the promise of love.

Rachel looks pale as she continues to share what Willow has told her about "the family." The women were encouraged to satisfy the men's sexual desires; doing so was considered the law of love. "I cannot count how many men I had sex with," Willow told Rachel, detached from her feelings.

This is a love story from the dark side, where love is the prelude to domination, where women and children become objects for others' whims or pleasure. I smell captivity, a place where women and children are not safe.

Willow needs to understand that this was not, in fact, love. When one's voice, sexuality, or integrity is subjugated in service of sex, that is exploitation, not love.

Rachel looks shaken. "I really like Willow," she says. "Is this what all my cases will be like?"

It is my job to ease these postgraduate fellows into this world, where what they understand about love, relationships, and goodness will be turned on its head. It is my job to help them find their best and most honest selves, and to guide them to form relationships that can repair their clients' pervasive injuries from love gone wrong.

"Willow's experience is so heartbreaking and yes, extreme," I tell Rachel. "Most likely, Willow was part of a cult where sexual abuse was not just accepted but encouraged. All your clients will not be like this. But too many will know about abuse that masquerades as love."

Chapter 9: CHILDREN FOR SALE

Jessica is in her early fifties, a fact at odds with her youthful appearance. Her long, straight brown hair rests on her shoulders; her face is flushed, as though she has just returned from a vigorous hike. She is determined to examine and overcome her past, not for its own sake but so she can lead the life she wants to live.

She has an advanced degree in public policy, but she works in a coffee shop. Jessica refers to the drinks she makes as "coffee sculptures." On occasion, she volunteers for the Red Cross, going to the sites of natural disasters for two or three weeks to help out where she hopes she can make a difference.

Today Jessica brings a video she wants me to watch with her. It's a documentary about human trafficking. "It is about young girls like me," she says.

"Okay, we can watch it together," I tell her. We go to the training room, where I pull down the screen and place the video in the player.

I feel anticipation and dread as I hand Jessica the remote control. "Any time you want, you can press this red stop button and you can stop or pause the tape," I tell her. "You can stop it any time, after two seconds or a few minutes." I want her to be able to determine the pace and to know that she can decide how much of the documentary we see.

I pull up my chair next to hers. I know this will be difficult to watch. It will test both my defenses and hers. This knowing and not knowing about horrible things, this precarious balance we keep, will be disturbed.

I am the witness to the stories of crimes and atrocities my clients experience. I try to avoid the quicksand of grief—their grief, my grief, grief for other abused children. Jessica and I are both gentle, angry women. My palms are sweating.

Children for Sale is the title of the 2004 documentary. The narrator, a white man in a dark grey suit, comes on the screen. He is poised, clean-shaven, with a news anchor's polished-for-prime-time voice. I immediately hate him.

"It's at exotic vacation destinations where horrendous crimes go on behind closed doors. Children, some as young as five years old, are sold as slaves for sex." His words are crisp for dramatic impact. "Tonight," he continues, "we venture into this dark place where sexual predators can gain access to terrified children for a handful of cash."

A snapshot flashes on the screen, showing four young children sitting on a couch in a dingy basement with cement walls. The scene of the crime is a small village with dirt roads, twenty minutes outside of Phnom Penh, the capital of Cambodia.

The predators who are involved in this despicable activity are mostly Americans. They are doctors, lawyers, and regular guys "on vacation." Sex tourism is what the commentator calls the crime.

I ask Jessica if she wants to pause the tape. She shakes her head no.

I want to stop the tape. I want to say, "Did you hear what they said? Children sold for sex, younger than five!" I want someone, everyone, to be shocked, outraged.

The tape continues. A human rights activist appears on the screen and says, "These children are sexual slaves; it is a crime against humanity."

The commentator reappears. "Now we go to a café that is a brothel." He walks down a back staircase and through a curtain of beads to where the girls wait. A woman explains, "Virgins are an extra attraction; $600 and you can keep them for three nights."

Jessica finally presses stop. I am relieved. We leave the training room and walk back to my office in silence.

My face is flushed from sadness and rage. I tell her I found the documentary hard to watch. She seems pleased to hear and to see that I am disturbed.

"I like hearing those words, like 'brothel' and 'sex crimes,'" she says. "I felt a kinship with the girls. Can we watch more next week? I tried to watch this with my husband, but I couldn't. I like watching it with you."

Three years ago, when Jessica first came to therapy, she was having nightmares. Her traumatic amnesia about her childhood was giving way to fragments of memory. This phenomenon of repressed and recovered memory, once a controversial topic, is now better understood.

In 1996, Jennifer Freyd published *Betrayal Trauma: The Logic of Forgetting Childhood Abuse*. Her research led her to a simple, intuitive, and elegant truth: children who are abused by a parent or caregiver they are dependent on are more likely to experience the loss of memory about their abuse. "A child's ability to detect betrayal may need to be stifled for the greater goal of survival," she explained. "A child who distrusts his or her parents risks alienating the parents further and thus becomes subject to more abuse and less love or care."

Children resist the knowledge that their primary caretakers

are dangerous because it is psychologically unbearable. This is particularly true for children like Jessica, who have no adult they can trust or turn to for help.

We also now understand that trauma that is not conscious does not disappear; it presents itself again and again until the past traumas are named and then tamed. Jessica's marriage is where her unprocessed trauma appears. In her marriage, she is emotionally whiplashed by the force of her unspoken past. Her marriage has been a constant source of distress and confusion.

From the age of nine to fifteen, Jessica was brought by her sociopathic father to "the house," where men paid to have sex with girls. "I was a prostituted child," is how she now refers to her ghastly abuse. She realizes that dissociation allowed her to believe that she had a good family. She did not always remember the abuse perpetrated by her father and "the men at the house."

Jessica fought the idea of being a victim; she hated her powerlessness.

During our therapy, the wall of Jessica's amnesia begins to crack; it does not tumble into pieces, but it is gradually disassembled, almost brick by brick. Jessica begins to recall the torture she endured as a child, and the earth begins shifting under her feet. Not quickly; not easily. Parts of her are frightened and resist knowing the truth of her past. She moves in and out of denial, touching the pain and grief and then retreating.

One day, Jessica draws a picture with the crayons I keep next to the table where she sits in my office. "This." She points to a line she has drawn between a man's legs. "This is the knife they stabbed me with."

"What is it like to start to remember the abuse that you experienced as a child?" I ask.

She replies with a single word: "Shocking."

It is difficult to imagine how memories of such consequence can hide so successfully. It is difficult to imagine being shocked by your own story.

Today in Group, Jessica tells the others that she is remembering horrible things about her childhood.

"How do you get these memories?" Kristy asks. "I can't remember anything about my childhood."

Jessica replies as if the answer is so obvious: "I see Laurie."

"But what does Laurie do?" Kristy insists.

"I don't know. We talk. Sometimes I draw pictures. We talk about stuff."

"Does she hypnotize you to help you remember?" Kristy pushes for a more satisfying answer.

"No," Jessica patiently replies. "It's hard to explain. It took a long time, but I trust Laurie. I never trusted anyone before." This is the trust and attachment required to safely examine memories that were too dangerous to remember before. Jessica looks at me and smiles.

The process of understanding and confronting a history of ongoing abuse is long, painful, and sometimes tedious. Trauma survivors need to feel safe so they can tolerate the traumatic material. That is trauma treatment 101. The paradox, the ongoing conundrum, is that a survivor's past teaches her that relationships are a source of betrayal, not of comfort. Jessica has never known a safe, reliable adult. She has no evidence that if she tells someone about the horrors of her abuse, she will be believed. Like a baby colt learning to stand on her new legs, Jessica's trust in me is shaky, fragile, and prone to collapse under stress. She wants and does not want to know what happened to her.

Remembering has many barriers. Who would want to know that their father was the architect of their ongoing abuse? Who could bear to know that their father made money from the torture they endured? Who could tolerate a household where love and tenderness were nonexistent?

When she was five, Jessica told a neighbor that her father was hurting her. "Your father is a nice man," the neighbor replied. "Now go back home; your parents will be worried."

Before Jessica found the words "prostituted child" to describe what happened to her, she would call the location "the house with the scary men." Much of what had happened there was a secret that she kept not only from others but also from herself. Sometimes she wondered if it was really a story about another little girl rather than about her; other times she was engulfed in nightmares and woke up startled, her nightclothes drenched in sweat.

Jessica begins to draw more pictures during our sessions. At first she draws purple stick figures of men whose hands have sharp objects on them instead of fingers. A little person with big eyes and long hair is surrounded by faceless green stick figures with no eyes. Over time, Jessica begins adding words to her drawings. Next to the small child, who has concentric circles of red and black in her belly, she writes in red crayon: "*This is a bomb inside me that's going to explode. I hurt inside.*" At the bottom is a pencil drawing of a penis. Next to it she writes, "*disgust gross sick. I am filled with anger and hate.*" In the left-hand corner is a stick figure with red tears and the words, "*Where's my mom?*"

Jessica shares her pictures with me. I, too, try to find words. Horrifying. Painful. That little girl is so frightened, so alone. Jessica is allowing me to be a witness to her abuse.

Jessica is still in pain most of the time. Sometimes I feel helpless in the midst of her overwhelming distress. We talk about safe places. Jessica loves the water, so I teach her to visualize the ocean when she is afraid or overwhelmed by her feelings. She practices yoga, and learns to calm herself when the memories flood and distress her. This remembering is hard work; it is not for the faint-hearted.

Jessica's drawings become more colorful, and the people

gain distinct features. The girl in her drawing wears a polka dot shirt and striped pants. Jessica draws with a new confidence, like a runner who has found her stride. She creates a vase to hold all the tears of the children. Jessica is grieving the childhood she is beginning to understand was hers, and the loss of the fantasy childhood she has constructed.

Chapter 10: LOVE AND LIES

When I was eight, I decided to fire my mother. I decided she was unfit for the job. My mother was a poor little rich girl, which I mean in the fondest way. Hiring others to care for her children was a legacy she inherited from her well-to-do family. When my mother was a child, a chauffeur drove her to school, a nanny took care of her daily needs, and a tutor helped her with her studies. To complete the romantic picture of her deprivation, at age nine, she had a pony of her own. Her pony, Bobbie, was her best friend. Not unlike me, my mother adored her father and felt distant from her mother. There was nothing evil or cruel about my mother. With many unmet longings of her own, she just wasn't fit for the job.

I have no memories of my mother near a stove; she did not know how to work the washing machine. She preferred fashion and sports to taking care of children. She was prettier than the other mothers. Her closet was filled with the latest fashions; she was a star on the golf course, and lit up in the presence of handsome and powerful men. I wanted a real mom like my friends' moms, who made them dinner and tucked them into bed at night. I decided that if I did not matter to her, she would not matter to me, either. Who needs a mom anyway? I perfected my indifference to my mother.

"How was your day?" she asked.

"Okay," I responded.

"What did you do?" she probed.

"Nothing," I replied.

"Where did you go after school?" She kept trying.

"Nowhere."

I deprived her of the privilege that belonged to real moms: the privilege of knowing the intimacies of your daughter's daily adventures, wounds, and triumphs. I believed that hurt her, and it secretly pleased me.

Try as my mother did to be part of my life, I moved from a child to a girl to an adolescent, and the door remained shut. Though she occasionally knocked, I was relentless in my indifference to her occasional motherly gestures.

My older sister, on the other hand, did not fire her mother. She was the queen of temper tantrums. She slammed doors when she was angry. At eight, she ran away from home (around the block with her stuffed animal). Many nights I listened to her cry herself to sleep. I hated when she displayed the needs of a child in search of a parent's attention. I wanted her to just give up, like I had.

As a teen, my sister hung around with the kids from the wrong side of the tracks—guys who looked like Fonzie, with tight pants and gel in their hair. My sister's white lipstick complemented the sticky hairspray on her hair, which she teased so it extended an extra two inches above her head. Slightly overweight, she poured herself into a tight black shirt. My sister's appearance drove my mother to distraction.

One fine afternoon, in front of our house with white shutters on Fox Meadow Road—we now lived in the rich part of town, where kids did not play kickball in the street—two police officers arrived with my sister and her friend JoAnne in the backseat of their squad car. They had been caught shoplifting a vinyl record at Alexander's, the discount department store.

It's not that I never shoplifted; it's just that I would never have gotten caught. But Susan had not given up on getting our mother to notice her distress.

Of all the pairing and possible constellations in my family, my mother and I seemed to be the worst match. Ironically, I think my mother and I were both plagued by loneliness. Both of us had absent mothers who were too absorbed in their own pleasures and needs to give the necessary attention their daughters. In this way, my mother and I have a deep connection to each other. We both knew the piercing, wordless loneliness of being a motherless child.

My father, meanwhile, had no use for young children. To him, young children were demanding, noisy, and smelled bad. He was not the kind of father who would change diapers or read bedtime stories. He was not the kind of father who sat down to help you with your homework. He loved a good time, though. He was lively and charming, a welcome relief from my mother. And when I was nine or ten years old, I realized I was my father's favorite. When I was with him, I could wear my shirt inside out, skip brushing my teeth, or eat a Tootsie Pop for breakfast.

My father's job required him to be on the road a lot. We learned to think of his time at home as a treat. When the front door opened and my father appeared, I barreled down the stairs at top speed and greeted him with a huge hug. "Hi, Monkey," he would say. In my father's world, everyone had a nickname. Mine was Monkey Face; apparently (and photographs confirm this) I had not been the most alluring baby, and the name stuck. But when my father sweetly called me Monkey, I conjured images of the adorable monkeys I saw at the zoo, and I felt more irresistible than homely.

My mother wanted us to have good table manners, dress nicely, and keep the house neat. Though my father and I never spoke about my mother's desires, he clearly delighted in my rebelliousness. I did not clean my room as my mother wished. I wore the same pair of blue jeans for weeks at a time, and I ate with my fingers whenever possible. My mother nagged me, but she was helpless in the face of my resistance. With my father's invisible wink, we became partners in our contempt for my mother's failings. He was more fun, more forgiving, and less concerned with the trivialities my mother nagged us about.

On weekends when he was home, my father took me to college football games (Princeton vs. someone). I loved watching the marching bands at halftime. My father and I ordered hot dogs. My father drank from the flask that he said helped him keep warm.

When winter ended and the warmth of the summer arrived, my father and I woke up early and headed to Mamaroneck Harbor. We stopped at the small, faded red shack by the water, bought worms for bait, and rented a wobbly tin fishing boat with a small motor. My father promised that if we found the prettiest spot on the lake, the fish would find it, too. On the water, with the sun on our backs, we sat mostly in silence and time passed effortlessly. I do not remember catching many fish. I just remember this precious time with my father, with no worries and where everything felt possible.

When I was in junior high, I frequently curled up on the couch next to my dad to watch the news. We both loved JFK. My father made me promise I would never date a Republican. I learned to like whatever he liked—football, fishing, and politics—although I did not share his taste for alcohol. Even though my father didn't take me to the circus or come to my birthday parties, when I was with him, I felt special, smart, and pretty. He was my best mirror.

At the beginning of high school, I began to date. Not because I wanted to, but because it was an unspoken requirement if you were one of the pretty ones. And I was the kind of girl that guys on the football team wanted to date. I had a thin, athletic body and green eyes that brightened against my fair complexion. My long hair was full of natural blond streaks that glistened in the sunlight. The boys began to call.

My father gave all the boys I dated nicknames. Alan, who liked theater, he called "the thespian." Marty became "Huck Finn" because of his adventures. Larry, who grunted at adults, my father simply called "the creep."

Each time I went on a date, my father waited up for me. He frequently asked me the same question: "Did you give him a little?"

I was unaware that this was not the standard greeting of a father to his teenage daughter when she arrived home from a date. Around this time, my father "kiddingly" began to introduce me to people as his child bride.

"I'm home." My voice echoed through the empty—well, almost empty—house. Bali greeted me with her tail eagerly wagging. I meandered into the kitchen and looked for something salty or sweet to satisfy my teenage hunger. I opened and closed the refrigerator. I tore open a bag of Fritos and spilled some chips on the cleanly scrubbed floor. I liked making messes, and not just to irritate my mother. I wanted to attack the lie of the immaculately kept house where everything was as it should be.

I walked up the carpeted stairs. Bali, tail still wagging, followed closely behind me. I drifted into my parents' master bedroom. In the alcove, almost a room unto itself, stood my mother's white painted dresser with its clear glass surface. Twelve drawers of varying sizes called to me. Her soft cashmere sweaters were folded neatly in the top drawer, her silk blouses in the next—a symphony of colors. In the small middle drawer, directly beneath my mother's underwear, was the drawer filled with her brightly colored scarves.

I wrapped one scarf at a time around my neck and looked in the six-foot mirror, imitating the elegant woman I thought I despised. The world of fashion belonged to my mother. My intrigue with this aspect of womanhood was hidden behind my contempt. I picked up the extra-long orange paisley scarf and draped it around myself, transforming it into an elegant dress. But the world of scarves and silk was distant from my adolescent reach.

Under the next scarf, one with green and gold threads, I discovered a white envelope addressed to my mother. My playful adventure into this world of silks and paisley suddenly shifted to a treasure hunt. I pulled out a handwritten letter with curly Gs and Qs. I hesitated for a moment, but my curiosity quickly trumped my reluctance to invade my mother's privacy.

"Dearest Betty"—I could not imagine my mother as *dearest* or *Betty*. The letter read like a page from a cheesy romance novel. My eyes lost focus. Words blurred into each other; *luscious skin, your lips, love, desire, mine, naked*, and various expressions of sexual desire I would never utter. It shocked my fifteen-year-old sensibilities.

Oh my god; my mother had a lover. I'd had no illusions that my parents had a good marriage, but affairs and infidelity were not part of the suburban fairy tale I thought I was living.

Once I knew my mother's secret, I developed a sixth sense for when my mother was on the phone with her lover. I would walk into her room unannounced, just to watch her squirm. When I did this, her phone conversation shifted abruptly, her voice became tight. Her warmth and gentleness was replaced with an awkward formality that signaled to the man on the phone that there was a child in the room.

When she hung up the receiver, I boldly asked, "Who was that?"

"Oh, that was someone from the orchestra where I volunteer," she lied without hesitation.

Lacking any subtlety or shame, I continued to torture my mother to the best of my ability. I picked up the phone downstairs to eavesdrop while she was in her bedroom. I needed her to know, even if it would never be spoken, that I knew her secret.

Truthfully, I felt very alone with this secret. I could not tell my father; it would destroy him. My sister was away at college, and my friends had real mothers who would never dream of doing such a thing.

My mother and I were in a silent war. I spoke to her as little as possible. I was withdrawn and cold as ice. I stayed away from the house until dark. I found endless ways to punish her for shattering my picture of marriage, for mixing love with lies. While the moon was bright, I crawled under my soft black and pink quilt. I hoped sleep would provide solace, but disquieting thoughts continued to intrude. I wondered what else was a lie.

Chapter 11: **THE TOPIC IS SEX**

The winter night encircles the room. Even more than usual,
Group feels like a retreat from the cold. The warmth of fellow
travelers creates a cocoon for two brief hours on this Wednesday
night. Tonight, the topic at the forefront is sex.

Wendy is becoming more courageous. Tonight she begins.
"I want to talk about relationships."

"That's a big topic," I say. "What were you thinking you
wanted to work on about relationships?"

Diana walks into the room five minutes late. Her knit hat
covers her ears and flattens her short, curly hair. Her fur-covered
boots reach up to her thighs. She looks warm and impenetrable.
"Sorry I'm late," she mumbles and takes her seat next to Kristy.

"When I was in high school, the other girls would say, 'Hey,
isn't that guy hot?' I felt nothing," Wendy says. "I thought maybe I
was gay, so I tried a relationship with a woman friend. It was nice,
but it felt like having a roommate you fooled around with once in
a while. I still felt nothing when it came to sex. I felt so abnormal.
I wondered if I had a frozen heart or some permanent defect."

The women in Group nod in sync like a chorus that was
just given their cue. Sexual abuse robs people of ease with their

sexuality and damages their understanding of how to create intimate relationships. Some people feel numb and shut down. Others feel the opposite and are sexually aroused easily and often. Both situations are problematic.

Diana takes her boots off and joins in. "I wasn't very sexual when I was a teenager, but once my stepfather was out of the house, I had sex all the time. I hooked up with older men, mostly in bars. They were toys to me, a night's entertainment. I always cared about my friends, but the men I had sex with I didn't give a shit about. But the truth is, like Wendy, I felt nothing. I can cut off my feelings with the blink of an eye."

"I know this is twisted," Wendy interrupts, "but what Diana is saying makes me feel less weird. Kind of like we are having normal—well, maybe not *normal*—feelings from being sexually abused when we were kids. It's funny how little I understood what my brother was doing to me. I always wondered, if someone just uses his fingers, is it still rape?"

Tonight, Wendy seems so vulnerable and trusting. I feel tender and protective.

"Unwanted sex that is forced is sexual assault," I tell her. "If someone uses their fingers or penetrates you with their penis, it is all a violation of your body and soul."

"Okay, that's good to know, but sad. My brother was usually drunk when he did it to me."

Carla looks at Wendy. "I am so glad you are talking about this. I think you're brave, and it's inspiring. I haven't talked much about this stuff either. My first sexual experience was with my cousin when I was twelve. He was nine years older than me. I felt really helpless. I knew I couldn't tell anyone because they would just blame it on me or brush it off. I still get flashbacks when I have sex with my boyfriend. Worse, now I get flashbacks when I breastfeed my daughter. I know she isn't doing anything wrong, I know I am choosing to have her at my breast, but these feelings come up and ruin the closeness with her."

I feel more and more heartbroken as each Group member talks about this residual damage they live with every day—their broken dreams, the interruption of their pleasure.

Kristy puts down the jewel-colored wool she is using to knit a hat for her daughter. "I am so sorry that those horrible experiences interfere when you are with your daughter. That is so unfair."

"Thanks, Kristy. I agree," Carla replies.

Jessica's eyes are wide open. Everyone is eager to speak about the topic that is often forbidden.

"I don't like sex with my husband, Harry." Jessica shares this like she is telling us about her dislike for Brussels sprouts. "Since we started couples' counseling, I told Harry that for a while I want my own bedroom and I don't want him in my bed. I told him I want to be the one to decide when and if we have sex."

"What did Harry say?" Wendy asks.

"He agreed he would move out of the bedroom while we are working on our relationship."

"Was he mad at you?" Wendy's eyes open wider.

"No, he understood that was what I need."

"That's remarkable," Wendy says. "How do you find a guy like that?"

"As long as we are on the subject," Diana interjects, "there is something going on at work that is kind of fucking with my head."

Diana tells the group about this man she likes at her job. "Tuesday about five o'clock, before we closed the office, he asked me to come to the storage room with him to get some things for the office. We walked down the wooden stairs to this large, cold room where file cabinets lined the far wall. Shelves with supplies are on the right. He looks at me longingly—you know how guys do that. Then he leans toward me and kisses me. He fondles my breasts."

The women are riveted.

"Then he unzips his pants. His penis was erect, ready to go."

Now the women in Group are either turning pale, or their

faces are flushed with a mixture of rage and fear, but Diana is cool and precise in her storytelling.

"I tell him, 'Put that thing away. This is not going to happen.' I say, 'You are a fool. You are married and your wife works upstairs.'"

The women in Group bombard Diana with what they have learned about abuse, saying things like, "You should report him," "That is sexual harassment," and "You can get him fired for that." And the statement they have often yearned for but seldom heard: "It wasn't your fault."

While the others frantically try to reassure and protect Diana, I notice that she is now smiling.

"You guys have this all wrong," she says. "I knew what he wanted when he asked me to go with him to the basement. I am not naive. I felt in control."

"Still, it was not your fault," they say, almost in unison.

Now Diana is angry. She feels misunderstood, unseen. "I will not let this man or my stepfather ruin my life. I am not a victim. I will not be prey. I had the upper hand, and I was in charge."

Diana feels that she called the shots. She feels pleasure in her triumph. She feels much more like victimizer than victim. And she needs the others to recognize her triumph.

When Diana was fifteen, the sexual abuse that had begun when she was nine came to a screeching halt. A nun tapped her on the shoulder as she sat attentively in her English class and said, "We need to go to the principal's office."

Diana was startled; her uniform covered her knees, she never swore within earshot of the nuns, her grades were good. She could not fathom why she was being pulled out of class; the principal's office was reserved for troublemakers.

Behind the large oak door, sitting on either side of the principal, were her mother and a policeman. Diana's mother had discovered her diary: pages filled with details of the ongoing sexual abuse perpetrated by her stepfather. She had called the police and reported her husband, Diana's abuser, to the police.

With her mother by her side, Diana was escorted outside to the squad car. They arrived at the station, where Diana was informed that her stepfather was in custody. Diana was asked for a statement, and then taken to her uncle's house.

Diana was spared testifying at the trial. Her stepfather was convicted and imprisoned, and remains so today.

The dark secret of the abuse was revealed, the truth was told, yet the damage from the years of her abuse remained. No one spoke about that day. Her stepfather's name was seldom mentioned again. So she turned to drugs and sex for comfort.

"I like to pick up guys," she says. "I'm good at it, and they are toys to me. I can fuck them and feel nothing." She says this with pride and only a hint of regret.

In victim or victimizer, the trauma of the past is repeated.

For Diana, sex is about power, not love. She cannot tolerate the tenderness, caring, or concern of others. But her mastery of men is leaving her lonely and secretly afraid at night.

"Diana, I understand your pride in your sense of control," I say. "You told your coworker in the storage room to stop. You did not freeze or check out. You were forceful and clear, and he stopped."

The woman in Group are shaken. They look to me for some relief or wisdom.

"Diana."

She looks at me. She allows me to hold her gaze.

"My wish for you is that you can have a relationship where there are no winners or losers, where there is tenderness and trust."

Diana is quiet. Her eyes soften just a little.

I notice the clock. Time raced by tonight.

I am moved by the authenticity of the woman in Group, by their courage to speak about hard things and to choose connection rather than silence.

"I think you guys are amazing," I say. My words feel inadequate. "Tonight was so moving, so intimate."

"What do you mean, intimate?" Wendy asks.

"You were honest, vulnerable, and compassionate. You listened to each other, honored each other's experiences. Real and connecting; that is intimacy."

"Hey guys, we were intimate. Pretty good!" Wendy's voice is lighter, playful, and hopeful.

"Thanks, Laurie."

"Yeah, thanks."

"We are lucky to have each other," I say.

They zip their jackets, wrap their scarves around their necks, pull on their gloves, and slip out into the winter night.

Chapter 12: TEACHING CHILDREN ABOUT LOVE

Why don't we take the time to teach children about love? Imagine if a teacher began a class by asking her students a simple question: "How do you know if someone loves you?"

The lucky ones might say, "When my daddy makes my lunch and puts my favorite snack in my bag," or "When my mom kisses me goodnight," or "Love is when your mom puts balloons all over the house on your birthday." Others, like my clients Kate, Jessica, and Suzy, would have darker responses, if they knew how to answer at all.

Kate never had a birthday party when she was a child. When she was six years old, she slept with a kitchen knife under her pillow. She was afraid that when her father returned home drunk, he would hurt her or her sister. She might say, "Love is when you hug your teddy bear and the house is quiet when your dad is asleep."

Jessica might say, "Love is when your older sister rocks you to sleep at night and whispers in your ear, 'It's going to be all right. Close your eyes. Just don't think about what happened; don't think about it.'"

Suzy would be unable to answer. She does not know how to tell when someone loves her. When she was six, she asked her grandfather, "Why do you touch me down there?" He replied, "Because I love you, but don't tell your mother."

Love is not just a feeling. Love is a promise, a commitment. We should teach our children that love is not about keeping secrets. We should teach them that love is not supposed to hurt or frighten them. Love relies on affection, care, protection, accountability, kindness, responsibility, and respect.

The teacher could write these words on the board and give the children copies of the list to take home. Love, she could tell them, must include a commitment to another's well-being. It is incompatible with abuse.

The students might not understand the meaning of all these words, but it would be good to give them a definition of love. Then, of course, the teacher would also have to *show* her students something about love, because children cannot truly learn about love with just words.

PART 2

"Whatever is unresolved and unsayable repeats."
—Annie Rogers, *The Unsayable*

Chapter 13: DISEMPOWERED

Elizabeth gingerly knocks on my office door. "Can I come in?" she timidly asks.

An oversized navy blue jacket disguises the shape of her body. The black plastic frames of her glasses overwhelm her face. Elizabeth appears deferential, apologetic for any minor inconvenience her existence might cause others or me.

I wonder what is hidden inside this disempowered woman. Extremes often have a counterpart: inside the submissive woman, a hidden warrior; inside the harmless puppy, a ferocious predator.

Elizabeth's fear and vigilance are ever present. She doesn't take comfort in the frame of therapy—the time, place, and privacy. For her, therapy is like a flimsy house made of straw that can easily collapse.

Elizabeth comes to therapy because her past intrudes in unexpected and mysterious ways upon her sense of safety. Like many others who experience prolonged abuse in childhood, some parts of Elizabeth know more about what happened to her as a child, while other parts of her are kept in the dark. This knowing and not knowing is a common feature of dissociation that protects the child from the unbearable losses and alienation.

When she remembers them, the fears from her past occur as if they are happening in the present. Elizabeth is plagued with flashbacks, night terrors, and unexplained startle responses.

"When I change my baby before I put her to bed I feel so much panic," Elizabeth says. "I check to see if there is blood in her diaper. This seems crazy."

Yes, it appears crazy. Because she cannot yet make the connection to the memories from a past that live in her body, that insist both on being known and on hiding.

"I think sometimes I keep secrets from myself," she tells me.

Therapy frightens Elizabeth. She watches my every gesture, anticipating humiliation and violations of trust.

Elizabeth needs a high degree of consistency and predictability. So to help her feel safe and enable her to recognize what is disabling her in her relationships, I make sure she encounters few surprises. Every time she comes for a session, she finds me waiting calmly in my overstuffed black chair. I end our sessions on time. I give her three weeks' notice if I need to miss or reschedule her appointment.

Elizabeth usually arrives slightly late to avoid spending any time in the waiting room. She tells me waiting there makes her fear exposure, humiliation, and shame. Over time, I learn that this concern is well earned. In Elizabeth's childhood, love and abuse were perversely intertwined. So although she hungers for connection with others, including me, she fears it will exact a high price.

Elizabeth's father was a diplomat. His job required that the family move frequently and live in unfamiliar cultures. Elizabeth does not remember a time when she attended the same school two years in a row. She recalls being in classrooms where the children spoke French and she spoke only English. Her parents believed this would be an enriching experience, but it fostered only estrangement and loneliness.

The isolation of living in foreign countries, coupled with a dearth of friendships to sustain her, intensified Elizabeth's reliance on her father. "He taught me about the beauty of music, introduced me to literature, and nurtured my love of reading," she tells me.

Elizabeth's mother was a successful writer who traveled to faraway places when she was researching her books. She wasn't someone Elizabeth looked to for comfort or affirmation. "My mother flaunted her accomplishments. She never acknowledged mine unless I got some trophy she could show to her friends," Elizabeth recalls. By contrast, her father was generous and demonstrative to Elizabeth, even at the expense of her mother. "On some level, my mother knew that my father preferred me," she says. "My father diminished my mother; he thought she was fat and unattractive, and he was not hesitant to say so. In my father's eyes, my mother did not fit the criteria for a desirable female."

Over time, Elizabeth begins to trust me and to trust herself more. One day in my office, a hidden part of Elizabeth appears. Elizabeth removes her thick glasses and places them in her lap. She is brash and oblivious to the effects of her words. "I like to fuck, and I am really good at it," she says. "My father taught me how to be the kind of female who knows how to please men." In this dissociated state, a part of her blurts out, "Imagine how special it is to have sex with the person whose sperm created you."

I feel nauseated. Horrified. I fear I might throw up. Her interpretation of her father's abuse and exploitation is shocking and twisted. Yet I am moved that I am being allowed to witness a part of Elizabeth that she herself barely acknowledges.

Elizabeth begins to remember: the sexy lingerie her father asked her to wear, the Christmas Eve when he said, "I think you are ready now. I have a special present for you."

Elizabeth cannot bear to see her father as exploitive and dangerous. Her attachment to him when she was a girl was passionate and fierce. So she has protected the illusion of being treasured and loved by him. Her ability to transform malevolence into something acceptable or even good is extraordinary. "I felt special with my father," she says.

The bond with one's abuser can be toxic, powerful, and seductive. When a beloved parent exploits a child's overpowering desire and need to love and be loved, the impact is tragic. Elizabeth transformed her father from the man who assaulted her body into a treasured lover.

Over time, Elizabeth develops the ability to feel tender, as I do, toward the wounded parts she secretly carries inside. She begins to draw pictures of herself as a child, coloring the fear and terror with reds, yellows, and oranges; she writes in her journals, describing to herself the forbidden stories from her past.

She begins to understand that her powerful compulsion to please her father had hidden her forbidden rage toward those who had hurt and exploited her.

The narrative about her childhood shifts. "I created an upside-down world where what's corrupt is good, what's dangerous is safe, what's evil is kind. It's an upside-down world that rips your soul and then you don't want to inhabit the truth," she says. Now she uses words like "incest" and "rape" when speaking about her father.

Over the next eight years, Elizabeth and I explore her hidden world. Together, we begin to understand the hopes, lies, and distortions that helped her endure and adapt to the unbearable. And in that process, the boldness and courage of the sexualized and exploited little girl gives way to a woman who is becoming whole and can face her father's betrayal.

The trust between us is deepening. Or so I think.

Chapter 14: BETRAYAL BLINDNESS

Denial protects us from knowing things that are unbearable. Denial makes it easier to wake up in the morning.

Things that are hard to know (from childwelfare.gov):
- One in three girls are sexually molested before age seventeen.
- One in six boys are sexually abused before they reach age seventeen.
- 90 percent of child sexual abuse victims know their abusers.
- 68 percent of child sexual abuse victims are abused by a family member.

Breathe, this is hard to know as well:
- Sex offenders who are not family members molest an average of 120 victims.
- More than 20 percent of children who are sexually abused are abused by age eight.
- Approximately five children die every day because of child abuse.
- 80 percent of these children are under age four.

Take another breath; we can do this:
• 5,000 priests have been identified and credibly accused of sexually violating minors.

"Nice" people abuse children.
It is natural to want to turn away.

———

We want a benevolent world. We want to believe the best of people, see the goodness and turn away from cruelty and betrayal. If what we see threatens our desire to be loved or the illusion that we are loved, we may transform malevolence into kindness, sometimes even idealizing those who injure us. Malevolence takes a bite out of our souls.

Tales cloaked in denial have gentler story lines; their characters are more pleasing. But denial makes us and our children vulnerable, destroying our ability to distinguish malevolence from benevolence. There is much at stake.

When a positive early attachment with a good or good enough caretaker is present, we experience relationships as a source of comfort. This is the foundation for developing the capacities and skills necessary to thrive in future relationships. The infant cradled in the arms of a loving parent knows a safe haven.

For an infant or developing child, attachment equals survival and abandonment equals death. Betrayal trauma occurs when a trusted person, someone a child depends on, abuses them. To acknowledge the abuse by a caretaker is incompatible with the child's desire to experience love and the necessary attachment to thrive. Our normal instinct is to be aware of harm, mistreatment, or injustice. But for those who experience betrayal trauma, our recognition of abuse or the extent of the harm being done is trumped by our need to maintain the relationship with our caretaker. "Betrayal blindness," a concept developed by Jennifer Freyd, is a way of not knowing that shields a child from an unbearable conflict.

I hear this in my clients' stories and how they evolve over time. When Jessica first came to therapy, she said she had nice parents who loved her. This was the fantasy that sustained her. When Elizabeth first spoke of her father, she described him as attentive and loving. To acknowledge his malevolence was at odds with her instinct to survive. Freyd's research shows that children who are abused by a parent or caregiver that they depend on are more likely to forget their abuse than those who are abused by people they depend on less.

Children are alert to injustices against them. "It's not fair" is a child's mantra. But if what we see threatens our desire to be loved or the illusion that we are loved, this capacity vanishes. We will transform abuse into love and idealize those who injured us. How could Jessica have survived if she had fully acknowledged her father's malevolence and the abuse and captivity she endured?

Trauma occurs when too much is happening for our psyche to survive and process. Isolated in her terror, Jessica had no one to turn to for help or support. She could not tolerate knowing and feeling the chronic fear and devastation. So she split off the traumatic events from her awareness. This process, called dissociation, allows an escape when there is no escape (Putnam, 1992).

Dissociation has many forms. Jessica experienced a type we call "traumatic amnesia." She simply didn't remember her abuse.

Others, like Elizabeth, experience a kind of dual awareness, knowing and not knowing, remembering and not remembering, at different times. Or they may remember what happened to them as children but experience the memories as if they happened to someone else, their feelings and the impact of the trauma remaining out of reach.

Diana knew her stepfather sexually abused her. She recalled the abuse in her home and in hotel rooms when her stepfather accompanied her to swim meets. But she minimized the impact of the abuse. She was numb, hardened against the pain of both betrayals: her stepfather's abuse and her mother's failure to notice. Before entering therapy, Diana was able to feel and express only one feeling: anger. She did not seek tenderness in her relationships. She sought control and power, the opposite of the powerlessness and domination she felt as a child.

Wendy was raised believing that the world was a dangerous place, and that family provided love and comfort. The abuse and neglect she experienced and witnessed in her family left her with no way to assess who was safe and who was not.

Betrayal blindness impairs children's ability to accurately perceive danger in relationships, making them more vulnerable later to abusive behavior by their lovers and partners. It causes them to dismiss or ignore the red flags that warn us about danger or about relationships that are likely to lead to bad outcomes. This blindness serves to protect the child, but at a cost.

Little Red Riding Hood is a wonderful example of the dynamics of betrayal blindness. Red lives on the edge of the forest. Her mother tells her to take a basket of food to her ailing grandmother, and warns her to stay on the path and not talk to strangers. As she skips through the forest, she meets the Big Bad Wolf.

"Where are you going, little girl?" asks the wolf.

"To my grandmother's house," she answers.

This is when I start wondering what's up with her danger detector. Are there really friendly wolves in the forest? I don't think so. "Get help!" I want to scream. "Don't talk to wolves!" This is also how I often feel with my clients who have damaged danger detectors. They ignore warning signs and do not recognize seedy characters.

Little Red Riding Hood then tells the wolf where her grandmother lives. "Mistake! Don't tell a wolf where your grandmother lives," I think. And then comes a truly mind-boggling display of betrayal blindness: She arrives at her grandmother's house to find the wolf pretending to be granny, and does not run straight out the door.

"Oh, grandmother," Little Red Riding Hood says to the wolf. "What a deep voice you have!" And then, "What big eyes you have!" and "What big hands you have!"

Here's the problem: Little Red Riding Hood and others with betrayal trauma are unable to scream, run for the door, or call 911 because they need to maintain a relationship with someone they cannot escape. They are under the spell of someone who hurts them. Their inability to assess danger and summon appropriate self-protective responses puts them in peril. This is the spell of dissociation.

Why is Little Red Riding Hood walking in the forest by herself? Does her mother ignore the existence of wolves and other dangerous beasts? Can Red acknowledge that her mother has put her in harm's way? And why is Red's father absent from the story? Are they pretending Red has a perfect childhood? Is that how Red became blind to danger and unable to distinguish a nice man from a beast? Perhaps this is how she learned to ignore the dangers of sharp teeth and hands that paw at her.

One of the cruelest truths about childhood trauma is the way it revisits its victims when they are adults. People who are victimized as children are more likely to be victims of domestic violence or to be sexually assaulted as adults. This is a consequence, I believe, of a child's traumatic experience of love. When trauma is not healed, when it remains outside of awareness, it drives the traumatized person to recreate the very condition that caused the wound. The trauma repeats, with tragic outcomes that baffle my clients.

A romantic notion I detest is that "love is blind." Love created with our eyes fully open and our past understood has a better chance of enduring, and of sustaining and enriching our spirits. In this way, another adage, "The truth will set you free," applies. But what my clients and I know is that the truth is also dreadfully painful.

Chapter 15: SURRENDER

My teenage body was definitely changing. My breasts gently peeked out from beneath my cardigans. I brushed my long, golden hair a little more often. My thin, strong body still brimmed with the energy of a girl who once effortlessly climbed to the top of our crabapple tree and loved playing kickball in the street. To others, I seemed ready for the world of boys and flirtations.

Bruce, my first boyfriend, gave me his ID bracelet. In eighth grade, an ID bracelet was a status symbol, branding you as somebody's girlfriend. At the time, all this required was talking to a boy on the phone and kissing behind the swings after school. Truthfully, I would rather have played kickball in my old neighborhood than be initiated into this world of boyfriends. To make matters worse, Bruce was annoying, and his ID bracelet was too small for my wrist.

My next boyfriend, Kenny, was an improvement. I loved the smell of the Dentyne gum he constantly chewed. He was the star of the school basketball team, and I was a great fan of the game—I played on the girls' basketball team from third grade until high school graduation. The basketball court was a happy place where all that mattered was my teammates and a round ball.

I missed my father, who was away more often than not on business trips. My mother and I were engaged in our version of the Cold War. Boys, for reasons I did not fully understand, were interested in me.

By the time I was in high school, the cool older guys my sister was supposed to be dating were asking me out. Boys thought I was pretty. I went to parties, attended proms, and held hands at the movies with a series of good-looking guys: football players, the president of the student council, the lead of the school musical. I necked in backseats of cars, smoked cigarettes, and laughed at guys' jokes.

I did not know why these guys asked me out. I wondered if there was a list of girls they were supposed to call, like salesmen who needed to make their monthly quotas. They did not want to date me because I was a great conversationalist; I was quite shy. And I didn't have a reputation for being easy. But I knew it was supposed to be a great honor to have cool, good-looking guys ask you out. And it never occurred to me that I could turn down dates, that I could say, "No thank you, I prefer the company of my friends or my dog. Maybe in a couple of years I might be interested." I would have easily given it all up to have a real friend.

One Saturday night, Lyle, a football player with red hair in tight curls that gripped his scalp, picked me up for our first date. If my father had been home, he would have nicknamed him "Red" or "Curly." Lyle invited me to a party to celebrate his team's winning game against Eastchester. I knew little about Lyle, and he knew little about me. We walked to the blue, two-door Chevy he'd borrowed from his father. Lyle opened the heavy car door, and I slid onto the passenger's seat.

On the way to the party, Lyle drove through the forest preserve and parked his car. The pine trees were starkly silhouetted against the sky; it was beautiful, eerie, and silent.

Lyle moved close to me and put his arm around my shoulder.

Ick, I thought, and I edged back to my side of the car. He moved with me. *Oh shit, this is so uncomfortable.*

"How about we go to the party," I suggested.

"Let's stay here," he said, with no sign that he would be willing to negotiate.

He locked the car doors. I could feel my heart pounding through my wool sweater. He leaned into me and kissed my face. I pulled away, but he was not deterred. His hands found my breasts. No one had ever touched me there. I did not want this guy to be the first. I struggled, but he did not stop.

"Okay," I said. "Do whatever you are going to do." I surrendered in passive protest. My body went limp. His hands moved up and down my breasts. I did not kick or scream, but I made sure he knew that this was not pleasurable, just surrender to his physical strength.

I don't remember how long we were there. He pushed my hand to his crotch, moving it up and down his penis. My hand felt like it belonged to someone other than me. My shirt was ripped, but my underpants were untouched. I guess I got off easy.

"I want to go home," I said when it was over, tears running down my face.

"I'm sorry," he said. "I hope I didn't ruin the night."

When I arrived home, I was shaking. I crawled into bed hoping sleep might erase this night of surrender.

The next morning, my mother greeted me by the stairs.

"How was your date?" she asked.

"Fine," I lied.

"What did you do?"

"Nothing much. We hung out."

"That's nice."

I could never tell my mother what happened. She wouldn't believe me, and how could I explain why I was so upset? I didn't have any bruises, and anyway, Lyle had kind of apologized. What was so bad? I didn't feel mad, just dazed. There wasn't anyone to help me make sense of what happened. Telling someone might have made it worse. And besides, I was managing.

It was not the night with Lyle's unwanted hands on my breasts that haunted me. It was the loneliness that followed. I needed words—words like "sexual assault." I needed someone to explain that sexual assault wasn't just something that just happens to girls, that it is a crime. I wanted someone to hate that this happened to me. I wanted my mother to be brokenhearted because her daughter had been sexually violated not far from home. That would have changed everything.

I wish I could have wept with somebody who cared. Then I might have become a stronger, wiser, feistier me. I might have decided that I would never get in a car with a man I did not know well again. I might have reclaimed my strong body, enjoying its power when I whacked a hockey puck past the goalie. The click of a locking car door might not have evoked panic and reminded me of the moment everything changed.

Men—football players, regular guys—I now knew could use their strength to overpower and sexually violate girls with little regret. The world had become less safe; my body felt less like home.

I wish I could have told my mother. I wish I could have said, "My date was not okay. It was awful, and I was frightened."

Chapter 16: ANOTHER BETRAYAL

When Jessica was eighteen, in a moment of lucidity, she decided to tell her friend's mother that she was being abused. But when she tried to speak, she became virtually mute; fear would not allow her to speak. She fainted, which alarmed her friend's mother. She called an ambulance.

Jessica was admitted to the hospital, but she was a puzzle to the hospital staff. With an empty smile and a pleasant demeanor, she shuffled through the halls of the hospital, afraid to speak. Within her were stories too difficult and too terrorizing to tell. She had no reason to think that anyone would believe her story, even if she could find the words. At times, even she did not believe what had happened to her. She preferred the fiction that she came from a happy family. The "don't tell" messages were embedded in her psyche, placed there by her father's threats, her mother's indifference, and even by her sister's efforts to protect her by chanting as she rocked her to sleep at night, "Just don't think about it. Just don't think about it."

Jessica was hearing voices inside herself—voices fighting to speak but terrified to do so. Jessica awoke in the middle of the night screaming, her T-shirt soaked in sweat. She remained in the psychiatric unit for two years.

Jessica's psychiatrist visited her every day. She found his long ponytail and casual dress comforting. The men who had frightened her in the past wore suits and were clean-shaven. Harry was different.

"I liked talking to him," she says. "He listened to me and asked me questions about how I was doing. He spent more time with me than he did with other patients. Before I went to bed, he would stop by and check on me. His pale blue eyes seemed kind."

After a couple months in the hospital, Harry took Jessica to his office. She remembers the tweed brown carpet, mahogany desk, leather chairs, and smell of Lemon Pledge. "That's when he first kissed me," Jessica says. "I didn't really mind. He didn't hurt me. What I did mind was the sneaking around; that made me feel dirty."

Her therapy sessions continued in the privacy of his office, and often included sex. Jessica had only a vague sense that this was outside the acceptable boundaries of a doctor/patient relationship. At age nineteen, she knew little about healthy boundaries; she had never known an adult who was trustworthy or protective.

How could she know about love or about caring? Her father was the architect of her abuse, a pimp for his daughter, using her for his own gain and maybe perverse pleasure. Jessica was a child for sale, her father the salesman. Her psychiatrist was kinder than the men she had known, but he, too, violated a sacred covenant with Jessica. He was the person who decided when and if Jessica would leave the hospital, if she could stay in the private, upscale hospital she was in or if she would be transferred to a state hospital. And in the hospital, Jessica escaped the tyranny of her father. She was in the hands of professionals who were supposed to help her with her fragmented identity, caused by years of agonizing abuse. But within the walls of the psychiatric unit, she gained another secret to keep, another violation of trust to endure.

As Jessica describes what happened to her twenty years ago, I am horrified by the sexual misconduct of her psychiatrist. I feel ashamed, as if the therapist who sexually exploited her is part of my clan, my community. I want to apologize to Jessica, but instead I say, "I am sorry, heartbroken, really, that your trust was betrayed."

Sexual and erotic feelings are part of being human. In the treatment of survivors of sexual abuse, these feelings are ubiquitous. They appear unannounced, unwanted, intruding into the calm of therapy, disturbing and frightening my clients and, at times, me. Understanding these feelings is an opportunity to redo something that went terribly awry in the past. It is an opportunity to safely reflect on forbidden sexual feelings, free from impulses and free from the threat of exploitation. It is an opportunity for the therapist to give voice to the feelings that were once unspeakable, part of a code of silence imposed on the abused child.

When Jessica's psychiatrist acted on his sexual feelings rather than contained and reflected upon them, the contract between client and therapist was violated and the original trauma was reenacted. Sexual contact with clients is forbidden, harmful, and against our professional code of ethics.

Jessica begins today's session talking about her husband. She wants to feel safe and to have a loving relationship with him, but she doesn't. "He triggers me," she says. "Sometimes I can't stand to be around him."

It is not unusual, when people are delving into a past of sexual abuse, for their relationships with their partners or lovers to be disrupted. Sex, closeness, smells, feeling aroused, the sight of genitals, all of it can catapult the survivor back to memories of their abuse. And Jessica has an additional challenge: she has been married to Harry—the psychiatrist she met when she was nineteen—for twenty years.

As Jessica learns about the boundaries that are necessary for healthy relationships, she is beginning to understand the beginning of her relationship with Harry differently. A therapist is not supposed to have sex with his clients, she realizes. Harry violated the ethics of the doctor-patient relationship. She is enraged, as if his transgressions just occurred.

"What were you thinking when you had sex with me when I was in the hospital and you were my doctor, my therapist?" she asks Harry.

"I was in love with you," Harry answers, as if that is a reasonable and clear explanation.

Jessica insists that Harry go to marital therapy with her to see if they can repair their marriage—a relationship that began with the violation of trust and safety. I give Jessica the name and phone number of my trusted colleague, a trauma-informed marital therapist.

Jessica considers ending her marriage. Harry panics. Jessica is the center of his world. Though therapy is unappealing to Harry, the one thing he is sure of is that he does not want to lose her. He keeps repeating, "I don't want to lose you. I don't want to lose you. I love you."

Every week for the next two years, Harry and Jessica take the train from their north-side apartment to an office building in downtown Chicago. Jessica is eager to expose the secret of the beginning of their sexual relationship. Harry is not. "Couldn't we just talk about our present relationship?" he protests.

"No, we have to talk about our past relationship." Jessica has a new strength and determination.

Jessica continues individual therapy with me, and she attends a weekly group therapy session with other survivors. Her voice has a new clarity and confidence. Even though Harry financially supports her, she insists on paying for her own therapy from the money she receives making "coffee sculptures" as a barista four days a week.

Harry has few insights into his past, but he begins taking responsibility for how he hurt Jessica. He is committed to understanding Jessica's traumatic past and how she still suffers in its aftermath. The therapist coaches him to become a safer and more supportive partner to Jessica. After several weeks of marital therapy, Harry apologizes in writing to Jessica for his transgressions when he was her psychiatrist many years ago.

There are many things Jessica and Harry enjoy together. They both love adventure, the outdoors, traveling to foreign places, and the thrill of scuba diving. But Jessica confesses that even though Harry is kinder and he has learned to listen to her, it is still difficult for her to be with him. "I still can't relax when Harry is in the house; my skin hurts," she says. "The thought of being close to him makes me sick. I keep thinking about all the times he intimidated me and made me feel bad."

"I can see that you don't want the marriage that you had with Harry," I say. "If you stay with him, you and Harry will need to create an entirely new marriage."

Jessica needs some space to decide what kind of relationship she wants with Harry. She needs to have what she has never had: a sense of agency and choice. She likes having options. She cannot say yes to love or to sex if she does not know that she also has a right to say no. She is also beginning to imagine a different relationship—one of equals—and realizes she cannot truly love Harry if she does not feel safe with him.

Jessica comes to her next session smiling. She shows me the finger on her left hand where she wore her wedding ring. "I took off my ring. I told Harry that if things get better, at some point he can propose to me. I told him that I need to have my own space, and then I asked him if he would move out of my bedroom into another room. And guess what?" She pauses, the edges of her mouth curl into a grin. "He agreed."

I smile too.

When Jessica first met Harry, she knew nothing about the boundaries that are required for a healthy relationship. She did not know that she had the right to refuse sex or any other kind of touch she did not want. She had no voice of her own. Now she does.

Chapter 17: YOU'RE MY FAVORITE

I did not dream of bridal gowns. I did not imagine a husband by my side or children I would someday nurture. Those things were for other people. They struck me as unlikely and frivolous. Love had become suspect and a bad bet for happiness.

It was the '60s. I dreamt about making a difference in people's lives and creating a just world. The Civil Rights Movement, the women's movement, and then the anti-war movement were my awakenings. I shed my plaid skirts for bell-bottoms and peasant blouses. In 1967, I left New York for college in the less exciting Midwest. Purpose, justice, and voice became my center, my identity. These things fueled my passions and guided my activities.

When I got to college, I found a handful of like-minded political activists. We talked politics endlessly, organized protests on the school grounds, and went to Washington for the larger gatherings. We bailed each other out of jail when necessary; we staged a takeover of the college president's office and handed out anti-war and student rights leaflets after the events of Kent State. My junior year in college, I went to Chicago to study and became a community organizer for a welfare rights group in Uptown, an impoverished neighborhood on Chicago's north side. I was happy. I felt part of something bigger than myself.

The wonder of the '60s was that I got college credit for most of my subversive activities. I graduated with honors and a major in political science. I never took a course in psychology.

My father delighted in my adventures. He had introduced me to politics at a young age, and it fit me like a glove.

After I graduated from college, I stayed in Chicago. Four friends from school became my roommates. I had a mattress on the floor and a cotton Indian bedspread that hung on the wall, covering chipped paint in the back bedroom of a two-flat. I got a low-paying job at a group home for pregnant teens. I could easily afford my quarter of the rent, buy as much brown rice as I desired, and pay for train fare to and from work. The Vietnam War was at full throttle: protest marches, sit-ins, and marijuana were our daily bread.

I loved it when my father came to Chicago on business. We would meet for dinner at the Four Seasons Hotel or the Cape Cod Room at the Drake Hotel—our two favorite haunts. The contradiction of appearing indifferent to wealth and status while luxuriating in it was one of the things I loved about being with my father. We were subversives, enjoying the extravagance of my father's expense account while preserving our rebellious temperaments. My father admired my radical politics and my passion. His favorite subjects to talk about with me were politics and sex. I much preferred politics.

At dinner, we shared our disgust with Nixon, and our outrage at the recent decision to send troops into Cambodia. The waiter, though reluctant to interrupt our lively conversation, took our order. My father knew my culinary preferences. He ordered for me: filet mignon, rare, with a baked potato and sour cream on the side. This pleased me; he was the best date imaginable.

My father then cleared his throat. With a hint of awkwardness his gaze moved directly to my eyes. "Laurie, you do know that you and Grandma Rosie are the two most important women in my life?"

His declaration of his devotion to me and to his mother did not surprise me. I took pride in my elevated status next to his revered mother.

My father put down his scotch; the mischievous glint in his blue eyes was gone, and he looked uncharacteristically serious.

"What would you think if I asked your mother for a divorce?"

I knew my mother and father had "stayed together for the children." They had fun together—they went to parties and on vacations, they both liked their alcohol and often drank together— but I saw little affection, no gentle touching or kissing, between them. And there was also considerable tension in our family: I had become my father's companion, and my sister had become my mother's. Now that my sister and I were both launched, why shouldn't he have some relief from a failed marriage?

I did not know to say, "How the hell should I know if you should get divorced?" At the time, his question seemed quite natural. I was still under his spell. Far from being disturbed, I was flattered to be his confidant. He was not divorcing me, just my mother.

When my mother found out that my dad had spoken to me about his desire for a divorce before he talked to her, she was furious with me. Why me? Why didn't she think, *Oh, Laurie, I am so sorry you were put in that position.* When did she forget that I was her daughter, not her adversary? And besides, why was she so upset? She had a lover waiting in the wings. She had betrayed my father for years while he was on the road making a living to support us. Was my father or our family more important to her than I imagined? Or was it just fear of change or the loss of financial security? Did she like the picture of family and marriage just the way it was, with her secrets neatly tucked away?

I didn't know. But whatever her reasons, my mother was distraught, and in her eyes I was a culprit—or at best a coconspirator—

in the demise of her marriage. By the end of that year, my father had filed for divorce.

When my father returned to Chicago three months later, winter had turned the skies grey and the winds howled. My father called me and suggested we meet at the Drake at seven o'clock for dinner. Before he hung up the phone, he mentioned that he was bringing a friend he wanted me to meet. I figured maybe he was stuck with some businessman he needed to impress or had invited someone he worked with whom he especially liked.

I drove down Lake Shore Drive, where waves crashed mercilessly against the Lake Michigan shoreline. The heater in my car was broken, the wind chill factor registered below zero. My wool gloves barely protected my chapped hands. I wrapped a plaid scarf around my face; my eyes peeked out from beneath it. I reached the glow of Michigan Avenue. Two blocks later, I turned left at the Drake Hotel.

I smiled at the valet, who suspiciously eyed my rusty car. I was not alarmed. I knew my father would make everything right and happily take care of my parking fee. The revolving doors opened into the lobby. The parade of chandeliers glistened with elegance. I followed the sign to the restaurant and bar.

My father put down his scotch and smiled broadly. Next to him, a pleasant-looking woman sipped her matching glass of scotch. She peered at me over tortoiseshell glasses. To my surprise, she smiled at me, too.

My father kissed me and said, "Hi, Monkey." I did not like that my father used his pet name for me in front of this stranger. My father then turned to the lady.

"Laurie, this is Annie."

She was dressed in a navy blue suit and a soft white blouse with fake pearl buttons down the front. She was not classy like my mother. She was flat chested, only mildly attractive. She didn't look like a businesswoman or a cheap date my father had picked up at a bar. We shook hands.

The maître d', in his black suit and shiny grey tie, escorted us to a table for three by the window and handed us each a menu. A white tablecloth, shiny polished silverware, and a candle graced its surface. My father turned to Annie and asked, "What do you want for dinner?"

What about me? Aren't you going to identify one of my favorite things on the menu and gallantly tell the waiter?

Maybe he was just being polite. I ordered for myself.

"So, Laurie, what are you doing in Chicago now?" Annie asked.

I was irritated with the intruder's feigned interest in my life. I tried to be polite, but her perpetual smile when she looked at my father or at me evoked my snotty rebelliousness.

"I work with troubled teens, and on my days off I'm trying to overthrow the government," I replied.

My father laughed, which pleased me.

Between the main course and dessert, my father paused for an uncomfortable moment. He looked at Annie, and then at me.

"Laurie, I have some news to tell you."

He smiled at me and so did she. Something felt weird and creepy. Then, like a storm that blasts from the sky without warning, my father said, "Annie and I are planning to get married."

The maître d' reappeared and asked to take our dessert order. I ordered some custard thing and excused myself. I walked down the hall to the ladies' room, where a white marble sink with a gold-plated faucet greeted me. I leaned over the gold-edged sink and threw up my dinner. I wiped my face with the fancy cloth towel. I returned to the table, dazed. My father and Annie behaved as if we were having a normal, pleasant evening. My stomach was queasy; the room was spinning.

Who was this woman who had seemingly appeared from nowhere? Had I really just eaten dinner with a stranger my father was planning to marry? *This cannot be true*, I thought. *It must be a bad dream.* Only months ago, we'd had our little chat about his desire to divorce my mother. How could he have fallen in love so quickly? During dinner, he'd said that they met on a business trip in Cincinnati and had fallen in love. Why was I not warned? Just, "Laurie, this is this woman I am going to marry."

I wanted to scream, to confront this madness, but I was well trained to suppress these impulses. My father and I had never fought or even had a serious disagreement. I was unaware of the price I paid to be cherished, to be his favorite. A charmed life with no conflicts, no accountability, and no difficulties was my father's wish, and it had been granted. I needed him. I adored him. I was the mirror that would never fail. "Mirror, mirror on the wall, who is the sweetest and most loveable of them all?"

My father never threatened me into being his admirer, his coconspirator, or his confidant. There were no ultimatums, no tantrums, no raised voices—just seduction, just the pull of maintaining my treasured position as his favorite. I was Sleeping Beauty in a trance. I had learned to ignore the parts of my father that were irresponsible, the part of him that hurt and deceived those he was supposed to love.

I felt betrayed, like a jilted lover. Had my father been cheating on my mother? On me? What the fuck was happening?

———

The day after my parents' divorce was final, my father married Annie. My sister refused to come to the wedding, so I was the sole ambassador from our family. Their wedding was small and informal, just me and a couple of their friends in a rented room in a hotel. I don't even remember where it took place; maybe in New York? I do not remember the ceremony, though I am sure no rabbi or other religious person officiated their union. I stood next to my father because I still thought that was where I belonged. Annie's beige silk dress held a corsage with white and yellow miniature roses. She stood on the other side of my father.

That day, I met Annie's two children for the first time. Debbie was two years my junior. Her long, black hair had a youthful shine. Her makeup was brightly pasted on her face. She smiled at my father in a way that confused me. She poured him a drink and stood too close to him. Michael, two years younger than Debbie, had a long brown ponytail, a badge of rebelliousness I admired. He looked like he could barely tolerate the evening. I immediately liked him.

What I did not know then, but would soon discover, was that Debbie and Michael had known my father for fifteen years.

———

I got sick like many of my clients become sick. It is a sickness that comes from secrets unspoken. It is the sickness of losing your voice to protect yourself. It is the sickness that comes when a child creates a fiction about the people who are supposed to love them. The cost of this fable is that we lose our authentic selves, or never fully develop them to begin with. Whether alone or in the presence of others, there is a hollowing loneliness. Furthermore, what we learn about love disables us later when we seek to develop relationships.

Here's what I wish I could have said at dinner with my father and Annie that night at the Drake: *Who the hell is this woman and where did she come from? What the fuck do you mean you are going to marry her? You are not sweet and lovable; you are a man who wants what he wants with little regard for others. You have seduced me into worshipping you. You eroticize your relationship with me. You spill, spit, and vomit your sexuality at me. I am a girl/ woman/daughter, and you treat me like your confidant, your pal, and your lover. Excuse me, Annie, or whatever your name is, I am leaving.*

I would have enjoyed at least a medium-size tantrum; maybe I could have thrown my water in my father's face, humiliating him in front of his fiancé. But that did not happen. Instead, I panicked, my sense of reality blurred. This could not be happening.

I stopped eating and allowed my father to bask in the delight of his new bride.

Love in my family was riddled with secrets, deception, and misalliances. The truth, with all its flaws and blemishes, is better. As a child, my feelings, my inner life, made no sense. The picture of normalcy my parents carefully choreographed was confusing. I wished I were from what they called a "broken home." At least then my sense that something in my family was very broken would have made more sense.

After I learned about Annie, my father was no longer my hero. I felt betrayed. The beliefs and illusions that gave me meaning collapsed. I was no longer the treasured one; my romance with my father had been ambushed. I was lost. I had no story of my own. I could not eat.

My dog, Frozo, a furry black mix of lab and collie, was my only source of comfort during that time. We took long walks together; she was happy just to be by my side. But one day, she slipped out of my apartment and vanished—and she did not return.

I hit bottom; depression enveloped me, an unrelenting emptiness interrupted only by occasional panic attacks. I did not care about myself or anyone. I was numb and had no feelings. I did not know who I was or where to turn. I continued to lose weight and looked more like a scarecrow than a young woman. I could not work. My doctor was alarmed and referred me to a therapist.

The psychiatrist's name was Dr. Duncan, I think. Her thick glasses made her eyeballs look big and distorted. I don't remember liking or disliking her. She said I was resistant to therapy. I don't remember that, either.

Dr. Duncan was an analyst, in the tradition of Sigmund Freud, whose personality evaporated into what was called a "blank screen" during therapy sessions. Her goal was to provide a canvas of sorts upon which her clients could project their conflicts, transference, and unconscious wishes. There was no person to be found behind Dr. Duncan's magnified glasses.

I, too, was a blank slate. I had no words for what I was experiencing.

Dr. Duncan gave me a medication to get rid of the prickly feelings that ran down my arms and other pills she said would help lift my depression. The pills made me sleepy and lethargic. The panic attacks lessened, but the depression did not budge. I had swallowed too many lies.

I grew up on Fox Meadow Road in an upper-middle-class family in a white house with grey shutters. That was true. My sister's name is Susan. True. We had a beautiful collie named Bali, also true. There was a mother and a father and usually someone else to take care of the house and the children. Mostly true. My parents loved each other and treasured their children; that is mostly fantasy. My father was always sweet and lovable. False.

Chapter 18: SOUP CANS

Growing up, Wendy had no role models for success but many examples of failure: two siblings dead from overdoses, a brother in jail, and a sister with two children who was on her third unhappy marriage. The odds were slight that many of the foster children Wendy had known and diapered were now leading successful lives.

Wendy was academically gifted and determined to end her family's legacy of trauma, violence, and neglect. She was determined to go to college, even though her mother wanted her to stay home and help take care of the foster children that revolved in and out of their home.

Wendy had no map for understanding whom to trust. She and her siblings were told to rely only on their family, where violence was ordinary, sexual abuse all too common, and neglect the norm. As a teen, she had no friends to chat with on the phone, giggle with about boys, or compare notes with about rock 'n' roll, clothes, or movie stars. She did not go to the mall or attend parties with loud music. She never brought friends to her chaotic house. And to seal her isolation, Wendy was given strict instructions to never talk to anyone about anything that happened in her family.

———

Wendy begins today's session with reflections about Group. "I am starting to like the girls in Group. I feel safer than I did at first. I am glad we're talking about relationships and sex, but it's still hard to admit things. The idea of dating freaks me out. I haven't gone on a date in twelve years."

"Twelve years," I calculate quickly. "Since you were in your early twenties?"

"Since my freshmen year in college, when I was raped."

I feel my heart pounding. "Oh, Wendy, I am so sorry that happened to you." I tell her that to remind her and myself that rape, though a tragically frequent occurrence, is a dreadful and traumatic assault on the body and soul.

She ignores my small expression of distress and compassion, eager to tell the story.

"My freshman year at college, I met a boy. He worked at the bar across the street from my dorm. I only saw him once in a while. He kept asking me if I would spend time with him, like have a beer or take a walk. I kept saying no. But he was really persistent. When I would get back from class, he would be waiting for me in front of my dorm."

"That sounds creepy, Wendy."

"He was just a guy. He didn't look creepy. He didn't have any scary tattoos or a sign on his forehead that said 'danger.' My friends knew him, too. I felt sorry for him." She pauses. "One day, he invited me to his dorm room. He promised nothing would happen, that we would just talk and hang out. There was something that didn't feel right, but I didn't trust my feelings. I wanted to be nice, and I didn't want to hurt his feelings by continuing to reject him."

I feel chills as Wendy describes this guy and the night she reluctantly went to his room. I can hear Wendy's over-exercised compassion obliterating her instincts to protect herself. She was trained at a young age to attend to the needs of others while no one protected or advocated for her. That night, she was repeating what she had learned. Others' needs and wounds took priority over her well-being.

"That night, he raped me. I was in shock. I could not move; I could not scream. What made it even worse is he smiled when he saw my blood on his sheets."

I am enraged; my teeth are clenched. *That sadistic bastard*, I think.

"I was afraid all that week that he would come back to my dorm," she continues. "I went home to visit my parents. I told them what happened."

"What did they say?"

"My mother said I should have known better."

"What an unempathic response," I say.

"My father was different. He cried and hugged me. I think it was the first time I ever saw my father cry."

"I am glad he was so affected and tender with you. He seems like he feels very protective of you."

"Yeah, he got some of his friends together to beat up the guy. It wasn't hard for them to find him; he wasn't hiding in the shadows. He kept working weeknights at the local bar like nothing had happened. After they beat him up, he left me alone."

Twelve years after she was raped, Wendy still lacks the confidence and skills necessary to determine if others are trustworthy. Without any experience of genuine love, she has no compass to guide her.

Wendy remembers her mother becoming enraged if Wendy or her siblings spoke to someone they did not know. Her mother was passing along her unprocessed and distorted fears from her own trauma-based beliefs about danger and safety. Wendy thought her mother was very protective, but the truth is she left Wendy very vulnerable. Because she was taught that only family was a sanctuary, and the world outside was where danger lurked, Wendy never learned how to evaluate people. And, in fact, her family was not a safe place. Her brother sexually abused her, she was physically and psychologically harmed by her older sister, and she witnessed life-threatening neglect and violence. All this occurred inside her home, not outside.

People who experience betrayals of this sort in their childhood are more than twice as likely to be victimized in adulthood. Many women who are abused as children, and then again as adults, wonder if there is a curse on them or if incidents of interpersonal violence are random injustices or maybe a cruel trick of fate. How unfair it feels to be so unlucky again and again, they think. In fact, they are suffering from one of the tragic consequences of childhood abuse. They are either overtrusting or insufficiently trusting, thus impairing their ability to protect themselves.

This damage to their ability to discern whom to trust is at the center of what needs repair.

After the assault, Wendy was unable to sleep and plagued by panic attacks. She decided to go to the mental health center. She had no words. Her counselor was patient. She did not want to pressure Wendy to talk; rather, she reassured Wendy that she could take as long as she needed to feel safe.

For months, Wendy said nothing. Then, one night, she awoke from a nightmare and called the counselor. In between breathless sobs, she told her counselor about the time she was raped.

"I am so sorry that happened to you," the counselor replied.

Wendy returned to the counseling center for her weekly appointments. She often fell asleep in the counselor's office. It was the only place she felt safe enough to sleep. This was Wendy's first experience of someone she could trust and look to for comfort.

In the years that followed, she immersed herself in her studies and avoided relationships. "I just keep busy," Wendy says. "I have three advanced degrees, but I have not dated anyone for twelve years. That is a lot of time lost that I cannot get back."

Wendy is beginning to trust me. I hope I can help her learn how to detect who is friend and who is foe, who deserves her trust and who does not.

Wendy leaves me a message the next day: "I finally decided I like you. So I guess for now, you are stuck with me."

———

The next week, Wendy brings me some pictures. "You asked what my house looked like, so I brought these," she says, taking a handful of pictures out of her briefcase.

I feel like an honored guest, invited into her family house.

"The first picture is of our basement."

I see a shelf about eight feet tall and eight feet wide filled with Campbell's soup cans. "Oh my," I say. "I have never seen so many soup cans in a person's house." It looks more like Andy Warhol's pop art than a pantry for feeding a family.

Wendy points to the corner of the picture where there are bags of clothes. "See this spot on the cement floor? This is where my father keeps his clothes."

Odd, I think, so I ask, "Is his bedroom near there?"

"Oh no," Wendy replies, "the bedroom is upstairs, but you can't move in it because it is so packed with things my mother collects. This is his spot in the house. There's a chest of drawers under the stairs. This is where he goes to change his clothes every day."

The next picture is of the living room. There is a large cage-like thing against the wall. "What is this?" I ask.

"Oh, that is for a canary."

"Isn't that awfully big for a canary?"

"Oh, yes. The canary was terrified in that big cage." She points to the corner of the picture and says, "That tank is for the tarantula."

I am being given a tour of her house of secrets, where Wendy was never allowed to bring her friends, where things happened that she was forbidden to talk about. It is more bizarre and disturbed than I imagined.

The next picture is of a room in the basement where books fill the wall-to-wall bookshelves. "My mother joins tons of book clubs. Books just keep coming into the house almost daily."

"Does she read these books?"

"I'm not sure; I know she has lots of duplicates. She has three copies of most of Dan Brown's books."

Still curious, I ask, "Now that most of the children have left home, do your mother and father have much money for collecting books and things?"

"Oh no. They are in debt. My father is over eighty and still goes to work every day. He sometimes tries to get my mother to stop spending money impulsively, but she gets mad, so he backs off."

I am witnessing what once passed for normal in Wendy's world. She is allowing me to see—and maybe allowing herself to see through my eyes—the disturbing environment she once called home.

Next is the picture of a room with more than 200 dolls in it. The weirdest thing is that the dolls are not appealing, not the American Girl dolls, but dolls whose eyes look empty and stare into nowhere. They are spooky—not adorable, not soothing.

Her mother's bedroom has a cradle near the bed with more dolls in it. The question that haunts me is why her mother took in so many kids. Were they like her dolls? Something to collect?

"This is really stunning," I say.

Wendy laughs. "You always say things like that. I can imagine my mother as a guest on the reality show *Hoarders*."

I am not amused. "This was your mother—the woman who raised you, the woman whose love was suppose to nurture you, who was supposed to teach you about trust and safety—not a contestant on a bad reality show."

Wendy can barely hear me. My assessment threatens to puncture her picture of the home she grew up in. I am careful to remember that these are the only parents she has, the people she has relied on for love. This is not an easy picture for Wendy to alter.

"So your mother collects a lot of things and junk," I tell her. "But when it was a house filled with children—your four siblings and up to ten foster kids at any time—that seems dangerous."

Wendy says, "Well, we had a bigger house then. And we had to have room for wheelchairs, which was good, because then you had to leave some of the floor clean so they could move freely. I was the one who tried to keep the house clean."

Next, in my Colombo style, I pose the forbidden question that continues to plague me: "Wendy there are some pieces of what you have told me that don't fit together. When someone adopts children or offers their home to foster children, they usually have some strong maternal instincts, they feel protective toward children and they want to provide a caring home for them. Your mother does not fit that profile. What do you think her motivation was when she took in so many kids who were in such need of care?"

"I think it was the money," Wendy says. Then she adds, "You know, you get more money for the crippled ones."

I am shocked by her answer—not because it seems unlikely but because she is willing to say these words. My stomach feels queasy. Wendy still is not as horrified by the things she tells me as I am. For now, I will hold the horror for us both as she begins—cautiously, reluctantly, painfully—to allow herself to know, to tolerate a new, devastating truth about her past.

I continue to ask questions that no one has ever dared to ask her, and that she is answering for the first time.

"Were you attached to these children?"

"Some of them, the little ones for sure. I loved the babies. I took care of them; I held them and changed their diapers. My sister would fight with my mom and then my mom would kick her out of the house, so I was the only one there to do it. I felt guilty all the time. I couldn't leave the house or turn my back on the young ones."

"I think you felt guilty because no one else did. Your parents should have felt guilt. On some level, I think you knew there was something terribly wrong."

Wendy doesn't disagree. We are walking together toward a different story.

"Someone eventually reported my mother; I forget why. DCFS closed down our house as a placement and all the foster children were taken away." She pauses then says, "I took good care of the babies."

"They were lucky to have you," I say.

Wendy gazes into space for a long moment. "Yeah, I guess they were. But I don't think I was that lucky."

"No," I say. "You weren't."

Chapter 19: MY FIRST MARRIAGE

My first marriage was not made in heaven. It was a partnership of two well-meaning souls with unhealed wounds from the past. There were red flags waving in the air, all of which I ignored.

The man with the beard and soft green eyes carried a bouquet of flowers. His two-year-old son, uncut, curly hair over his eyes, held a small potted plant that was tipped slightly to the right. As the boy walked up the stairs to my apartment, he left dirt on each step. This was my first date with Robert.

We went to a noisy Mexican restaurant two blocks from my apartment. After dinner, we walked home. The streetlights illuminated the musty city sidewalk. The boy, Matthew, began to whine and cry; it was late for a two-year-old. His father lifted him onto his shoulders; a smile returned to the boy's cherubic face. The pee that filled his diaper dripped onto his dad's denim shirt as he carried him.

When we returned to my apartment, Robert disappeared into the bathroom to change his shirt and Matthew's diaper. I sat in a big, comfy chair next to the radiator, which spat hot steam as it attempted to warm the room. Matthew walked out of the bathroom and crawled into my lap as if it were waiting for him. His hand reached for my hair and he began to twist a strand around his index finger. The thumb on his free hand slipped into his mouth.

Robert was funny and bright, and he cared deeply, as I did, about the abused and neglected children that the system discarded. His blue eyes twinkled with delight and mischief, yet just under the surface there was a distinct vulnerability. He appealed to me. The fact that this man was attempting to raise a child alone also pulled on my heartstrings.

Matthew had the appeal of a puppy. He was adorable and endearing with his curly brown hair. His slightly unkempt look evoked maternal stirrings that I had never felt before. And he and Robert were a package deal.

This duo had such promise, such charm, and they were in such need of a woman's love. I decided to audition for the job. Not that I knew much about love, or was well schooled in the ways of motherhood. But I was determined and passionate, and they were, too.

Robert's mother died when he was six and left him and his four siblings with his alcoholic father. His father, unable to take care of children, sent them to an orphanage. Robert's childhood bedroom was a large dormitory. The nuns on duty made sure that he and the others were in bed with lights out at the established bedtime. This was where he lived until he went to college. Robert entered adulthood wanting to create the family he never had.

By the time Matthew was born, however, his mother and Robert were heading for a divorce. Matthew's mother loved him, but she was emotionally unstable and did not feel capable of raising a child. Robert, who had long dreamed of a family, left the hospital with Matthew wrapped in a blanket, a single parent to a baby boy.

Dating Robert involved many challenges. One night, after a nice evening together, Robert and I returned to my apartment, and not long afterward I saw through the window that Robert's car was being towed. I imagined that he had parked in front of a fire hydrant or piled up too many unpaid parking tickets, but I was wrong. Robert's car was being repossessed. On the salary of a social worker, he was drowning in unpaid bills.

During the day, Robert had a demanding job as the director of a group home for disturbed kids with a never-ending series of emergencies: runaways, knives and guns hidden under beds, abrupt returns from unsuccessful home visits, short-staffed shifts. I didn't mind helping. I would pick up Matthew from day-care, and he would stay at my house until Robert got home. I found a playgroup for Matthew, one that encouraged cooperative play and more creativity, and he was happy there; the staff was attentive, and he made friends easily. I loved buying Matthew nice clothes from the secondhand store in a nearby wealthy sub-urb. Soon he looked well taken care of. His hair was out of his eyes, and he was no longer mistaken for a girl.

The three of us moved in together. I definitely was falling in love with Matthew, and I think with Robert as well.

One day, I arrived in the late afternoon to pick up Matthew at his playgroup. A female staff member in a tie-dyed T-shirt bel-lowed down the stairs, "Matthew, your mother's here."

"That's not my mother," Matthew said.

When we got home, I read Matthew his favorite story. "Fer-dinand the bull likes to sit under the shade of a cork tree and smell the flowers. The other bulls like to fight, but not Ferdi-nand. Even when Ferdinand is forced into a bullfight with a mat-ador, rather than becoming angry and attacking the matador, he stops in his tracks and smells the flowers the crowd has thrown into the ring." After I finished reading the story, Matthew looked up at me and said, "I want to be a flower when I grow up."

That night I said something offhand to Robert. Maybe it sounded critical to him, or maybe I interrupted him, but his voice suddenly changed decibels. A loud, angry voice spewed hurtful words in my direction. Robert's rage startled me; the vibrations of his anger stayed in my body and disoriented me. I did not think of myself as someone who evoked rage. I secretly expected to be adored, with little required of me.

Matthew turned to his father and asked, "Daddy, are we being mean to Laurie today?"

Though at times Robert was quick to anger, I excused his angry outbursts as a reaction to the stresses in his life. Most of the time, we enjoyed each other.

For several days, I dragged around the house, not my usual self. I felt sick to my stomach and listless. My flu symptoms came and went for the next two weeks. Over coffee with a friend, I complained about my lack of energy and queasy stomach. "I bet you're pregnant," she said. I quickly dismissed her flippant diagnosis.

She was right.

Having another child was not at the top of Robert's agenda. He had barely established equilibrium from the stresses of being a single parent. He was still plagued by unpaid bills. Our relationship was too new and uncertain to consider marriage. He was anxious, distressed, and angry. We decided we would see how things unfolded.

I was prepared to be a mother to this baby, regardless of the outcome of our relationship. Although the pregnancy was a surprise and definitely unplanned, I was pleased and excited about the life that was growing within me.

Robert, Matthew, and I continued living together. Robert attended birthing classes with me. We read Matthew books about where babies came from.

Nine months later, while baking loaves of banana bread, I began to have frequent contractions. Robert called his best friend, Sam, to come stay with Matthew while we rushed to the hospital.

Many hours later, I gave birth to our daughter, Emily. After an extended and exhausting labor, I kissed my daughter and handed the baby to Robert. He placed Emily on his belly. Robert and Emily fell asleep.

That night, Robert fell in love with his daughter.

The first weeks at home with the baby, Robert was as happy as I had ever seen him. Matthew was now three years old. There were two new rules in our house for Matthew: One, you cannot step on the baby. Two, you have to wear underpants when company comes to visit. I was hopeful that we were becoming a family.

Chapter 20: **DOG BITE**

The room is filled with anxious anticipation tonight. Everyone senses it. Kristy is sitting on the edge of her chair. Her hands are clasped; she hasn't brought her knitting needles, clay, or colored pipe cleaners to twist into appealing monsters. As the clock reaches seven, Kristy, like a racehorse waiting for the gate to open, says, "I want to start." She is never the first to speak.

"I have something I want to work on," Kristy corrects herself. "'Want' is not exactly true; I don't want to, but I need to."

She begins by introducing us to her dog, a two-year-old, 120-pound, furry black puppy. "Grindel follows me around all day. He lies at the foot of my bed at night, leaving little room for my husband. He wags his tail so hard when I come into the room that he knocks my coffee cup off the table, splattering coffee all over the carpet.

"Yesterday, Grindel was in his crate, chewing on one of my kid's toys. I put my hand in his crate to get the toy out of his mouth. He showed his large teeth and growled, and then he bit me. Blood dripped from my hand, dripped on my carpet. I feel so ashamed for letting this happen."

She begins to cry. Soon, she is holding her head and sobbing breathlessly.

The animal she adores turned on her in an unexpected moment. She is stunned, overwhelmed. I understand Kristy's sense of betrayal when her dog's animal instincts momentarily transformed him from her loyal pet into an aggressor. A dog is the essence of unconditional love for many who grow up in families where caring is in short supply. Their pet is a predictable lifeline: soothing, affectionate, and loving.

After a few minutes, Kristy stops crying and calms down enough to talk.

"It's not the dog bite," she explains. "It's that I couldn't recover, I couldn't stop crying. I began thinking about my father and my fear intensified. My father would wake me up in the mornings and slap me on the butt. No matter how much I protested, this remained the morning ritual. As a teenager, I would scream at him after he woke me, 'Fuck you!' So my relationship with my father was not a love fest. I disliked him and always thought he was pathetic."

Kristy is visibly angry; the energy of her anger overwhelms her earlier feelings of despair. But moments after she describes her father's assaultive and humiliating morning ritual, she collapses into sobs and covers her face again.

The members of Group wait until Kristy catches her breath. Then she describes a memory in detail, as if it had just occurred.

"I remembered my father came into my bedroom at night when I was little, about six. At first, I saw his face: his hair was messy from sleep, and I felt glad he was there." She is now sobbing between sentences. "Then I was afraid. And later confused. He came into my bed. I remember the sensation of his fingers in me."

I am there with her, feeling the fear, the violation, his fingers intruding in her child's body. Traumatic memories have a vivid and raw quality; they are less narrative than visceral.

The women in Group one by one respond to Kristy, speaking of times they have recalled shocking things from their past.

Some Group members express rage at her father and at all the fathers who violate their daughters.

When a parent or caretaker switches from being a benign or nurturing presence to an aggressive predator, it is a betrayal of momentous proportions. When her dog betrayed her, Kristy remembered for the first time her father's fingers robbing her of the sanctity of her body and dismantling the sacred trust between the two of them.

When Kristy was a child, she had no words to express what she felt, but she knew she did not want her father near her. She also didn't know whom to tell. Her mother, according to Kristy, lacked the maternal instinct to protect and nurture her children.

Traumatic memories often hide deep in our psyches, only to reappear when the body, mind, or senses are reminded or awakened years, even decades later. When she was a young child, Kristy could not consciously acknowledge the sexual abuse she was experiencing. Doing so would have left her in an unbearable state of terror and helplessness. Forgetting helps a child survive the disconnect between wanting love and protection from her parents and experiencing the opposite. However, when memories go underground, there is a cost.

My client, George, suffers from PTSD. He was working in the World Trade Center in New York during the September 11, 2001 terrorist attacks. He escaped to safety, but he remembers a smell like singed hair, and his fear and feelings of helplessness when he did not know if his colleagues were still alive.

Now George lives in Chicago and travels by plane to New York for his work. His panic attacks while flying are putting his job in jeopardy. It is easy to understand that planes to New York might activate memories and feelings of overwhelming terror for him.

Kristy's trauma, on the other hand, is not activated by planes but by relationships—by her desire for and fear of closeness. She is not afraid to fly. She is afraid to love and be loved. The damage from the abuse she suffered as a child forged a destructive path through her development, impairing her ability to seek and use loving relationships as a source of pleasure and comfort. This is the tragic impact of the unwitnessed losses from her childhood.

Tonight, Group is a mix of compassion, awe, and empathy. These women also know about betrayals, as well as the shock of remembering.

"You are brave," Nancy says.

Others nod.

"You inspire me all the time," Diana says. "You have such a big heart, and you have so much courage."

I ask Kristy how it was for her to share what she remembered with us.

"I get more support here than I ever got from my parents," she replies. She is quiet for a long moment. Then tears reappear and she struggles once more for words. "What surprises me— this is not what I would have guessed I would say, but the word that comes to me about sharing this tonight is 'beautiful.'"

"I wish I could do what Kristy is able to do," Carla says. "I can't talk about the sexual abuse that happened to me with my cousin. I mean, I always knew it happened, but I could never tell anyone or talk about it. I want to put it behind me; I want to feel safer with my boyfriend, and this abuse stuff keeps interfering. The times I've tried to talk about it in any detail, I've spaced out. When I went to a workshop here about sex and trauma, I fell asleep. I don't remember anything the workshop leader talked about after the first three sentences."

"I imagine there is a very good reason that you have so much difficulty talking about this," I tell her.

"Okay, but why? And what do I do about it?"

Her question hangs in the room.

Jessica says, "I have a terrible time when I begin to remember something from the past. My body remembers way before the rest of me can. I walk around scared and with this sense of dread for weeks."

"Carla, why do you think at nine you didn't tell anyone what was happening?" I ask.

"Because it would have made it worse and no one would have believed me. My mother randomly went into rages and beat us for things we didn't do. She called me a whore and slut when she was mad."

"Pardon the understatement, but it is clear that your mother was not someone you would look to for compassion when you were hurt or afraid," I say. "I am so sorry, Carla. You were so young, and what your mother said was so cruel and twisted. Telling would have been equally as, or more traumatic than, what was happening with your cousin."

"When I walked out of my house every day to go to school, I felt free, like I had escaped," she says. "I just put everything that happened at my house away."

"So talking about the abuse is like walking back into that house where you were so severely injured," I say. "Maybe you should trust, for now, that the part of you that does not want to or does not yet feel ready to talk about the sexual abuse should be respected and honored. I trust that when you are ready, you will be able to do more work on this. Tonight was a big step. You talked to us and stayed present; that was great."

Carla looks relieved.

Others congratulate her too. "I am so glad you are here, and what you talked about was really important," Wendy adds.

I am exhausted yet pleased. I believe the work Kristy and Carla are doing is healing. Dissociation—not knowing or denying the impact of what happened—is the wisdom of our psyches protecting us from devastation and sometimes even keeping us alive when there are no better options. But the path to vitality and wholeness requires an ability to tolerate knowing about one's traumatic experiences and the feelings they evoke. It is the path both Kristy and Carla must travel to be keep the nightmares of their pasts from haunting their present and future lives.

Chapter 21: MEETING NATALIE

After my parents' divorce, after the uninvited, flat-chested woman married my father, after I lived through a paralyzing depression, after the therapist who stared at me and gave me pills that made me sleepy, I met Natalie.

Or rather, my best friend Allie introduced us. Allie had wild, curly brown hair. She was funny and adventurous and smoked cigarettes. I was more restrained and cautious. Her moods registered on the manic side of the continuum, while mine hovered on the depressive side. But we were both seekers in our mid-twenties.

"There's this place where these two cool, famous therapists run a free therapy group every Monday," Allie said. "Let's go!"

About forty-five minutes north of Chicago, we found the sign—HAIMOWOODS—written in permanent marker on a piece of wood nailed to a tree. We slowly drove up the tree-lined dirt path, pebbles crackling under our tires, until we reached a concrete building with a bell tower that looked like an abandoned school or convent.

Inside, people milled around an oversized coffee pot and nibbled on something that resembled coffee cake. A thin woman in a simple skirt and an unremarkable blouse with coarse, curly hair untouched by a hairdresser greeted Allie and me. "I'm Natalie," she said. "Welcome." Her welcome felt more like one for treasured guests than for two hippies the wind had blown in from Chicago.

"We meet in there." Natalie pointed to the room down the hall.

Natalie had gotten her PhD from the University of Chicago, where she was a student of Carl Rogers, the founder of client-centered therapy. After graduating, she had become a student of Eric Berne, MD, the founder of transactional analysis, a social psychology that focuses on interactions between people as the key to unlocking and resolving psychological problems.

Berne was trained in traditional psychoanalysis. In 1957, after fifteen years of training, he was denied a position as a psychoanalyst at the San Francisco Psychoanalytic Institute. Within a year, he had written two seminal papers challenging Freudian psychoanalysis's basic premises and highlighting the value of interpersonal interactions over the mysteries of the unconscious. He, like many of us who were attracted to transactional analysis, was quirky, smart, and rebellious.

Berne was dedicated to creating a system of thought that demystified therapy and psychopathology. He invited his patients from the hospital psychiatric ward to hear his students present cases. He insisted that if the doctors or trainees could not talk about their patients' treatment and diagnoses in front of their patients, what they had to say was not worth saying—a simple yet radical idea. Berne challenged the elite, expert position of the therapist, which he believed diminished patients' dignity and their responsibility for make changes in their lives.

The radical tenets of transactional analysis appealed to my humanistic values and my commitment to social justice. TA, as it was known, empowered the therapist and the client. It also fit in with the stance of feminists who were challenging the traditional view of human development.

At the core of TA is a contract between the client and the therapist. It is not the therapist's job to diagnose what is wrong with the client and then fix it. Rather, the two collaborate to provide the focus and the direction of the therapy. This model challenged the "power over" dynamic of inequality and oppressive relationships.

I was enamored with Berne's insistence that the therapist decline the traditional position of "expert." A transactional analyst is trained to be an astute observer of how people communicate their feelings and beliefs in their interactions with others.

Natalie's national reputation as a TA therapist and trainer did not translate into fancy clothes or pretense. The group I was about to attend was free of charge. She and her husband Morris, also a transactional analyst, believed that everyone, regardless of their financial resources, deserved access to good therapy.

"Motley" is the best word for the people who filed in for the session: farmers' wives, who I imagined had just left their aprons on the counter; therapists in training from France, who had come to study with Natalie and Morris for a month; a man with a long salt-and-pepper beard; a black taxi driver who'd driven his cab there from Chicago; a large white man who had just been released from a psychiatric ward; several of Natalie and Morris's students; and Allie and me.

There was no distinction between therapists and clients in this group; everyone was expected to participate, offer what they knew, and work on their own issues. There was no hierarchy, no distinction between professionals and non-professionals. No one was more ordinary or more special.

Natalie started by asking, "Who has something they want to work on?"

The man with the salt-and-pepper beard, who turned out to be an unemployed storyteller, raised his hand. "I want to work on something."

This was not the first time he'd been unable to find work,

he said, but now he was in danger of losing his apartment. "I want to find work and support myself."

Morris asked him if there was a part of him that did not want to go to work.

"Oh yes," he said with pride and energy.

Natalie and Morris always noticed energy. They believed where there was energy, change could occur. "Tell us about that," Natalie encouraged him.

"I worked in my father's butcher shop from the time I was eight years old. The shop stank from the smell of manure. It was repulsive. I wanted to play by the stream or go fishing like the other kids. If I complained, my father beat me."

This man, who looked like he had slept in his clothes for a week, moved me. My eyes were glued to the storyteller. Natalie moved an empty chair in front of him and said, "Imagine your father is here. Can you tell him how you feel?"

"I am afraid to tell him," he replied.

"Tell him that," she said.

I thought she eloquently avoided evoking the man's shame.

He began to speak to the empty chair. Soon he began to cry, to sob. He sounded like a young boy. "I loved you. I wanted to please you. But I was really little. I wanted to play with the other kids, not be stuck in the shop all day."

Now Natalie asked the man to switch chairs and be his father.

When the man became his father, he switched into Yiddish and began to yell. Then something changed; a tear ran down his face. Natalie noticed. She asked the man to ask his father why he was sad.

More Yiddish, but his voice was softer this time. I was mesmerized.

"My father said he was sorry, that he needed my help, that he was afraid of losing everything, and that we would all starve." A twinkle returned to his eyes.

"Now," Natalie said, "put your eight-year-old self in the chair. Can you talk to him about work?"

This time he spoke in Yiddish to his younger self.

"What did you say?" she asked.

"I told him that we would not starve, that he could play and work. I told him that telling stories was joyful."

He smiled. It was clear that soon we might see the storyteller's name on the marquee of a club in Chicago. I hoped he would take a shower before his next performance.

I did not talk that first day. I listened, watched, and noticed. What amazed me was the mixture of laughter, kindness, sorrow, and hope that emerged. I felt part of something I did not yet understand. I just knew I wanted to come back.

I returned several more times. At first my heart beat faster when I contemplated saying the words, "I have something I want to work on," the cue to get Natalie and Morris's attention. But eventually I began to respond to others and even talk about myself.

Inspired by my humbling experience at the group home where I recognized I was sorely unprepared for the job. I decided to go to graduate school and pursue a degree in psychology.

Psychology and the practice of psychotherapy were radically shifting. Encounter groups, Carl Rogers's client-centered therapy, Fritz Perls's gestalt therapy with the double chair technique, and Jacob Moreno's psychodrama had changed the traditional notions of treatment. Concepts like unconditional positive regard, empathy, here and now, body awareness, mutuality, and empowerment captured our imagination in the late '60s and early '70s. The analysts, with their notepads, their devotion to the mysteries of the unconscious, and their blank expressions, did not inspire us. Our training incorporated all the new, cutting-edge theories and approaches with the enthusiasm and chaos of a new movement.

During my graduate program, I learned more about new, experiential, and contemporary therapeutic approaches. But unlike my experience with Natalie and Morris, I did not feel I was in good hands. I felt as though I were among cowboys who privileged adventure and new experiences over safety and construction of a trusting therapeutic relationship.

After graduating, I returned to Natalie and Morris to join their TA program. They trained their students not simply to become transactional analysts but to become artists. They required all their students to participate in therapy groups as patients. They believed that therapists had to do their own personal work in order to gain the skills, awareness, and integrity necessary to meet their standards.

I attended and participated in the Monday therapy group and then the supervision group. We read and studied the theories of TA, and in the process discovered the wounds, life scripts, and lessons learned in childhood that currently affected us. I felt privileged to witness and experience the work of two gifted therapists as I learned the skills of my trade.

Natalie and Morris were my mentors, and Natalie was my therapist. Today that would be considered a dual relationship and ill advised, but in the 1970s it was not uncommon. Natalie's role as my mentor and as my therapist did not seem problematic; in fact, I felt twice blessed. Once a week, I drove up the winding path to attend two hours of group therapy followed by two hours of training and supervision. Each week, I was greeted by the smell of coffee and freshly baked something-that-resembled-coffeecake.

Natalie's brown eyes were radiant from the brightness of her mind. Whenever a therapist presented a case in supervision, she would ask us what our question was about the treatment. She did not spoon-feed her students or indulge us in a pedantic hypothesis about a client; she insisted we think for ourselves and say what we needed. If we did not formulate a question about our case, she would either wait or come back to it later, but she was never harsh.

I was unaccustomed to the discipline Natalie required. At

first, I resented it. I had been both indulged and neglected as a child. My material needs had always been met, and little had been expected of me in return, though many of my emotional needs had gone unnoticed. Natalie, in contrast to my parents, was neither neglectful nor indulgent. I came to admire her brilliant mind and her gentle, fierce strength. If she had a blind spot, it was that she was unmoved by victims; she was not a fan of needless suffering. She preferred, or rather she treasured, feistiness over surrender in the face of adversity.

Natalie was highly regarded in her field but uninterested in flattery. One member of the International Transactional Analysis Organization once commented that she believed Natalie was the most ethical person she knew. Natalie was unwavering in honoring the ethical guidelines of her profession, yet unafraid to break the rules when she believed it was in service of a client's well-being.

Mondays, as required, I continued in the group to work on my issues. One day, I began by saying that I'd had a weird dream I wanted to talk about. I unabashedly described the dream, unaware of the obvious and embarrassing wish it revealed.

"Tell the dream in the present tense," Natalie requested.

"I come to group, and Morris announces that his co-therapist is dead and he is in need of a replacement. I wonder whom he will choose, hoping it will be me. I am so embarrassed."

I suddenly realized the blatant meaning of the dream. My unconscious wished to kill the mother and take her place. Couldn't I have had a dream with more subtlety?

Natalie turned to me warmly, without contempt or concern about the revelation that I subconsciously wanted to off her, to compete with her, to win the battle that I had previously won over my mother at great cost. She asked, tenderly, if I wanted to co-lead the group with Morris for the day. She offered me her chair and sat next to me. I led the group with Morris, and Natalie visibly took delight in my skills and insights.

Natalie saw in me the wish of a child longing for the adoration of her father, a girl who also needed a mother who did not see her as a competitor. Natalie, unlike my mother, took pleasure in my growth and successes. She delighted in my affection for Morris. I felt safe with Natalie, but even more important, she made me feel safer in myself.

Something else began to change. This motley group began to feel like home. Our collective wounds, the laughter, and Natalie and Morris's guidance transformed us from a collection of distant souls with different values and lifestyles to a community of shared humanity in which everyone mattered.

Chapter 22: GROOMING

Today, I would rather be with my client Cynthia, who thinks I am trustworthy and talented. I am the best therapist she knows, and she has known many therapists. Or Mary and Tony. He is verbally abusive at times and she is hypercritical, but I maintain an alliance with both of them, confronting and nurturing them while modeling good communication. If there was a video camera recording my work with this couple, I am confident my students would watch it with admiration.

Instead, here I am with Dan, and my skills feel inadequate.

Dan waits for me to fail him. His trust is paper-thin. He scrutinizes my every nuance, the tone of my voice, my posture, noticing almost imperceptible changes in my expressions. I can inadvertently hurt him, which he can ill afford, quite easily. Sometimes he wants to know I care about him, but if he believes I'm indicating that he is special, he becomes terrified and enraged. I am in a double bind with Dan, one created by his abuse: indifference is mortifying and affection or empathy feels like dangerous foreplay. Gestures of affection and caring confuse him, but he does not want to live without love. In the ways he tries to love, the trauma repeats itself.

Before Dan was betrayed by his abuser, he experienced prolonged, deliberate grooming, a cunning and skilled seduction. This is a common pattern in childhood abuse of boys. The perpetrator might help the child with his homework, counsel him when he is in trouble, or teach him to play baseball. The abuser may lead a double life, being a pious man of the church or working in a soup kitchen when he is not abusing boys. The double life is a powerful tactic for predators. Their socially responsible behavior in public causes parents to drop their guard and allow them access to their children. They do not look or act like people one might suspect sexually terrorizes children. Most people would respond with disbelief if they were told what was happening.

Worst of all, such predators create a situation in which the victimized children are fond of them. The boy likes the attention he gets. They have fun together, share great moments, and play games together. The predator is everything you would want in a father, friend, or companion. Gradually, there is touching. The boy may be young, four or five. It does not hurt when the man, his friend, touches his genitals. The sensations confuse the boy; his body responds. The boy wonders if this kind of play is okay. This man, his trusted friend, tells him that what they are doing with their bodies is about love. The trusted man's penis is introduced into the play, slowly, carefully, not too scary at first. The boy has no words to tell what is happening to him, and even if he does, he thinks, *Who would believe me?* This is what happened to Dan.

Grooming exacts a cruel cost: love and caring are the preamble to the crime. Empathy and caring, the primary tools of my trade, remind Dan of being groomed by his abuser when he was a small boy. He worries that my caring and empathy may also be the prelude to more betrayal. The trauma appears between us so it can be understood, and so we will create something different.

When Dan feels affection for me, he wants to destroy me. He is aroused by my presence. Today, I notice that he is staring at my breasts. I am very uncomfortable, and I feel slightly threatened and quite vulnerable. We are alone in my office with the door shut. I fight my speechlessness. I gather my courage and say, "You are staring at me."

"Yes," he says. "I was noticing that your right breast is slightly larger than your left one."

The fear in my body intensifies. I acknowledge to myself that I am scared and feel violated. I calm myself so I can reflect and think about what might be happening or being acted out between us.

Is Dan showing me something he cannot tell me? I wonder if Dan wants me to know the fear of being in the presence of someone who suddenly turns a safe moment into something frightening and unsafe.

My task is to be trustworthy and to teach Dan how to be trustworthy himself. It is my job not to reenact with him his abusive history, with him in the role of perpetrator or of victim. I do this imperfectly and with great difficulty.

Therapists often say that they want to work with victims of abuse, but they do not want to work with perpetrators. This is an imaginary dichotomy. Victims and perpetrators do not come in individually wrapped packages. Victims victimize, and perpetrators are often wounded souls.

The gender code prefers rough and tough boys, not boys who have been victimized or sodomized. Boys are supposed to fight and resist, so they disown abuse and minimize its destruction. But their hidden shame is corrosive, and the toll of the abuse is more likely to be enacted than shared in words in therapy, at least initially.

Dan is quiet; I can see something shifting in him. He looks young, and he no longer appears powerful or frightening. He is a bright man, and he is suffering. He wants to know love that does not hurt, love that will not injure him or the person he loves.

I ask him if his behavior a moment ago was due to his desire for me to feel what the abuse was like for him.

He stops and looks up for a moment, then says, "Yes. I want someone to know what it was like."

"I can imagine how frightening and confusing the abuse must have been for you. You were so young, so trusting. A man you trusted violated your child body and spirit. He abused you and showed no regret."

Initially, Dan's feelings of shame, confusion, excitement, and rage intrude in code between us. Over time, we find words for the unspeakable and the unspoken. We decipher Dan's story, and he learns to monitor himself. He stops making inappropriate sexual comments. I feel safer, and I think he feels safer, too. He does not want to be a predator or a victim of abuse.

I am helping this man, who was horribly abused, learn about trust and love. Dan wants to be a good man and a good partner. Sometimes he is, and sometimes he is not.

Chapter 23: NOT FOR COWARDS

This work is not for cowards. It is not for nice therapists who avoid feelings of fear and powerlessness. It is not for therapists who feel compelled to share themselves excessively with their clients, nor for those who withhold the depth of their caring, empathy, and compassion. It is not for therapists with rose-colored glasses who insist on a benevolent world without cruelty or evil. It is not for therapists who fear awakening their own demons.

We therapists want to be helpful, gentle, and compassionate. We want to admire and be moved by our clients' courage. But trauma and abuse require more from us. The harsher feelings evoked by trauma disturb our picture of ourselves and challenge even the most seasoned therapist. Sometimes we are rendered powerless and stripped of the most precious parts of ourselves.

When a traumatic past is dissociated, disavowed, or denied, the story is alive but unspeakable. Unconsciously, nonverbally, my clients convey their unspeakable feelings and experiences to me. Our clients require us to listen, to read between the lines.

People do not venture into my office with their stories of childhood abuse clearly outlined, complete with details. Often, their stories appear as snapshots, pulsing with sensation but incomplete. They are two-dimensional, lacking the emotions my clients feel are too dangerous for them to express. And some clients don't even have a story to tell, because acknowledging their past is too much to bear.

Untold stories continue to haunt my clients. They appear in the lives they go on to lead or not lead. "I want a family," Wendy says when we first meet. "If the stork would just drop a baby on my doorstep, that would be great. Relationships terrify me. I haven't gone on a date for ten years." Her untold story intrudes on her dream of a family of her own.

The stories may appear in a startle response—when the door bell rings, when the sweet smell of pancakes filling a kitchen reminds my client of the breakfast she ate the morning before everything changed.

The stories may also emerge in night terrors. Jessica turns to sleep for a reprieve from her constant anxiety, but she is awakened by nightmares night after night, her nightgown drenched and her heart racing.

Most importantly, untold stories are enacted in the therapeutic relationship. My clients show me what they cannot tell anyone, and it is my job to understand what my clients are showing me—to hear the stories that appear between us, the stories that beg to be known and understood. This occurs over time, sometimes slowly and sometimes suddenly.

In my work with trauma survivors, I have felt an array of emotions that surprise and startle me. I have felt emotionally numb at times, enraged at others. I have felt violated, captive, and even stalked. Such a spectrum and intensity of feelings is part of being a trauma therapist. We experience the full range of human emotions our clients evoke in us. But we have a different set of skills and capacities. We must be able to contain and reflect on our feelings of rage, fear, love, eroticism, compassion, and grief, and understand them in the context of our clients' deep relational wounds.

The art of this work begins with a keen mindfulness and inner listening. Our job is to allow ourselves to feel, to pay attention. I reflect on my inner experiences and put words to them for my clients: fear, violated, startled. This practice of inner listening and naming of inner experiences detoxifies feelings that seem dangerous. We can teach our clients that feelings are not dangerous, that actions are what injure.

Chapter 24: THREE WET KISSES

The knock on my office door annoys me and startles my client. I decide to ignore it and continue our conversation. There is another, more insistent knock. I open the door a crack and find Lucy, my next client, peering back at me. She is fifteen minutes early for her appointment.

"Oh, I'm sorry," she says, "but you don't have a 'Do Not Disturb' sign on your door."

"I will be with you in a few minutes," I reply and shut the door.

Later, I walk into the waiting room, where my intruder is waiting. "Hey, Laurie," Lucy begins. "Can I give you some advice?" There are three other people in the waiting room who are now studying the patterns in the carpet to avoid eye contact with her.

Without pausing, Lucy continues, "Those books on your shelves are too high to reach. How about getting a stool or a ladder? And do you know you have hot water for tea, but no cups? Also, there are three signs on the door pointing to the new waiting room. Don't you think one sign is enough?"

I quickly corral her into my office, maybe to protect her from the scorn of the others in the waiting room, or maybe to protect them from the contagion of her agitation.

"You know, the other teachers at school are really pissing me off," she begins before I sit down. She speaks gruffly about several incidents at work where a younger teacher said something that offended and hurt her.

"I feel so dissed by them," Lucy says. Her self-esteem is held together with the fragility of paper clips and bubble gum. "Do they think I sit on my fat ass all day?" Slowly her anger and gruffness fade into a look of exhaustion. "I get so tired," she says, more softly now. "My brother, Teddy, you know the one who is sick? He is not doing well. Now he can barely chew his food anymore."

I haven't seen Lucy for two weeks. I notice that her greying, usually undisciplined hair is shorter, a little neater than it was last time. She has also replaced her old briefcase, which bulged on every side, with a nicer, larger one.

Lucy's brother, Ted, has a terminal illness. This has forced her and her four siblings to try to rally as a family. This is not something they know how to do. Their attempts are fraught with moments of tenderness followed by misunderstandings, outbreaks of anger, and loud fights. They know little about how to care for themselves or each other, or how to be a family.

Lucy's childhood was, at best, unstable. Her mother had bipolar disorder, and her father left her and their four children when Lucy was in grade school. "I think Ma had it rough after Dad left; honestly, she was never herself again," she tells me.

Lucy's mother answered the phone when her sisters' boyfriends called and flirted with them. "My sister says that Ma once had sex with one of her boyfriends," she says. "My dad was nuts, too. He would visit sometimes. One day, on the stairs that went down to the basement, he kissed me and put his tongue in my mouth."

Lucy tells these startling snippets from her life with the indifference of a student reading aloud in class. She knows that her mother was largely unable to parent due to her manic-depressive episodes. But Lucy is dissociated. She does not connect the facts with feelings, or acknowledge the crippling impact these events had on her.

As our session comes to an end, Lucy claws through her briefcase, pulling out papers, a brush, and other miscellaneous objects to find her checkbook. She writes me a check, puts it on the table, and gets up to leave.

Usually, I sit still in my chair as Lucy leaves and I wish her well. This time she asks if I would give her a hug. I am not averse to hugging clients when they request it, but when people have been physically and sexually violated, I am always mindful and assess if it is a good idea for this particular client at this particular time. Lucy does not know much about boundaries that foster safe relationships. Today, though, I am aware that she is grief-stricken because the loss of her brother is imminent. Her vulnerability moves me to respond. Cautiously, I get up to give her a brief hug.

Lucy presses her large body against mine and grips me in a bear hug; she begins to stroke my back. Then she places three kisses on my earlobe. I instinctively wipe the saliva from her wet kisses off my ear.

"You have really helped me," she says as if what just happened was a normal and pleasant interaction. "See you next week." She walks out of my office.

I am speechless, which is uncommon for me. I feel gross, assaulted, and slightly aroused, which is most disturbing.

These are the forbidden feelings that therapists often deny. These are the moments that are fraught. What has occurred between me and Lucy is unsettling; it is the unprocessed trauma appearing in code. If I can tolerate and accept what I am feeling, I may find access to the wordless experience Lucy is attempting to share.

In the middle of the night, I awaken thinking about our session. *Did that really happen?* I think. *Is it normal to caress your therapist and kiss her earlobe?*

I have a strange desire to think that what happened between Lucy and me was not a big deal—a slip, maybe just ignorance of personal boundaries. I want, as Lucy must have wanted with her mother and her father, to ignore it or minimize it. I want to act as if it never happened. I pride myself on being the kind of therapist who does not shy away from speaking the unspeakable, but I am stunned and have temporarily lost my balance.

Lucy has shown me what is, for her, still an unspoken experience from a family in which perceptions of reality collide with normal expectations. Your mother is not supposed to sexually proposition your boyfriends. Lucy's mother violated the boundaries between mother and daughter, daughter and peers, without regret or acknowledgment. Your father is not supposed to casually French kiss you. Lucy's family was a confusing and chaotic place where the most basic boundaries, roles, and expectations were not honored.

It is also a violation of boundaries and roles to caress your therapist and kiss her on her ear. My own denial and minimizing of what happened that day—my first instincts—help me understand the strategies Lucy used to survive her upside-down world.

When she kissed my ear, Lucy showed me the experience of her childhood. It was a clue to the story that remains too difficult for her to grasp. Her desire, the desire of many abused and neglected children, is to maintain a picture of a parent who loves them, even if it is a false image with important details missing. The absence of love is a curse that exacts a toll most children find unbearable. Betrayal blindness—transforming the malevolence, cruelty, or damage inflicted by a parent into something palatable or ordinary—is the creative act of a child seeking love. Lucy has shown me what she does not know about love and about the boundaries necessary to keep children safe.

It is my job to be the midwife to Lucy's story. It is my job to share my account of what happened and my desire to ignore or minimize the significance of it with Lucy, just as I believe she must have done in her family. If my shame interferes with my awareness and acceptance of my uncomfortable feelings of arousal and disgust, if I disown or deny this odd moment between us, I may inadvertently distance myself from Lucy or shame her for her inappropriate behavior. Instead, my empathy for her deepens and so does my understanding of the unpredictable and frightening world she had to navigate as a child.

It is my job to do no harm. The next session, I will talk to Lucy about what happened between us, about the story she has helped me understand. When our session ends, we will gently shake hands.

Chapter 25: NO SURPRISE

When Emily was two and Matthew was five, Robert and I decided to get married. Matthew wore a corduroy jacket with a white shirt and blue jeans. The ruffled top of Emily's leggings was on display as she twirled to show off her pretty purple velvet dress. In my best friend's living room, surrounded by friends and family, we said our vows. In the dining room, a three-tiered wedding cake with white icing stood on a table, strawberries neatly placed on each layer.

When we went to cut the cake, the strawberries on the first layer were missing. Emily's face was painted with white icing; strawberry juice stained her cheeks.

The Chicago folk singer we hired began with two songs she had written for the children. I then requested "Wild Women Don't Get the Blues," which she belted in the great tradition of Bessie Smith. Everything was as I had hoped it would be; it was a joyous day, a cozy ceremony that allowed us to celebrate our new family with our friends.

The next week, in the chill of a winter afternoon, I arrived to pick up Matthew at his playgroup. A staff member greeted me and bellowed down the stairs, "Matthew, your mom is here."

I winced, anticipating Matthew's usual declaration that I was not his real mom.

Matthew walked up the steps, his art project in hand. With a big, toothy smile, he looked at me and said, "Hi, Mom."

I have been privileged to be "Mom" to this day.

We were becoming family. On Sundays, we went to the zoo, the circus, or a carnival. Group outings had been a high point of Robert's childhood at the orphanage. He introduced Matthew and Emily to roller coasters and he introduced me to family vacations.

Robert said he often felt like he was taking three kids out our Sunday excursions. This was true. My parents went on trips to exotic places, but they left my sister and me at home with the hired help. In summer, we were sent to sleepaway camp. I do not remember going to special places as a family, except when we visited our grandparents on holidays. I remember watching the Macy's Thanksgiving Day Parade from the thirteenth-floor window of my grandparents' Fifth Avenue apartment.

Weekday mornings, Matthew, Emily, and I walked five blocks to the bus stop. We got off at the Fargo and Sheridan stop. Emily and I walked Matthew to school, where the other first graders greeted him enthusiastically. I kissed him good-bye, and then Emily and I walked back to the bus stop. As we waited in the chilly Chicago wind for another bus to arrive, I distracted Emily with stories about my childhood dog, Bali. With our gloves warming our cold fingers and our transfers nestled in our hands, we boarded the next bus to the Howard Street stop, where Emily and I got off the bus and walked two blocks to her daycare at the YMCA. Then I walked back to the bus stop, waited for the next bus, and traveled eight miles to my office, where I saw clients until it was time to get back on the bus and pick up the children. This added three hours to my already long day.

It is not heroic to take your kids to school and daycare on the bus, even during cold and windy Chicago winters; actually, it is quite ordinary. But for me, it was charting new territory. I was being a parent whose commitment to her children took priority over other personal comforts or ambitions—an activity unlike anything I had experienced as a child. I was repairing an injury from a childhood in which my need for love and caring did not make it to the top of my parents' list of priorities. My sister's and my emotional and physical needs were outsourced to others.

My days were long, and Robert's were longer. He was working two jobs, and with our limited funds and Robert's debts, paying our bills was a constant stress. I felt like a rich kid with no money; Robert felt the humiliation of being poor. We both worked hard and took care of the children. But Robert was growing exhausted and depressed, and I was becoming lonelier.

Robert's temper began to escalate, and depression often followed. Sometimes, when he was angry, he hit or threatened Matthew. Afterward, he was overcome with shame. He wanted to be the father that he never had, attentive and loving. He wanted Matthew to be happy. When Matthew was happy, he felt like a good dad. When Matthew was not happy or misbehaved, and when Robert was tired, his temper flared. I hated his behavior toward Matthew.

I was also in a bind that often accompanies abuse. When I attempted to protect Matthew, Robert would punish Matthew harder. "Okay, if Laurie is such a good parent, why don't you just go live with her?" he said. The idea of losing his father terrified Matthew, who already felt the pain of the separation from his birth mother, whom he now only saw on alternate weekends.

Threatening Matthew with abandonment was cruel. I was frightened and worried about the impact Robert's behavior was having on the kids. I asked him if he would go to therapy with me. He agreed. Things got better for a time, and I felt relieved.

But other things went terribly wrong. Sex, for one. We were two injured souls, misreading each other. Our past injuries and traumas appeared, uninvited, in the bedroom.

One of my clients taught me the term "reluctant arousal."

She described the horror when her body would become aroused when her father sexually abused her. My father's sexual preoccupation with me pleased and frightened me. I, too, was afraid of desire—his and, unconsciously, mine.

For women to heal from sexually inappropriate and abusive experiences, they need to feel safe in their relationships. Communication with their partners is crucial. They need to learn to express their desires and be able to refuse unwanted sexual contact. But when I told Robert something I wanted or did not want sexually, he felt rejected and criticized. He would turn away from me, ending our lovemaking. My choices were to repress my own needs or be rejected. This replicated what I believed as a child. I could adore my father and not complain or acknowledge that anything was wrong, or risk losing my precious connection with him. As a child, the stakes were too high. I already felt disconnected from my mother; I could not risk losing my father's affection. This time, with Robert, I chose to have a voice and tolerate abandonment rather than be silent and compliant. I felt more whole, yet terribly rejected and alone.

Robert's vulnerability was also well earned. A Catholic orphanage is not a place to learn about the joy of your body or the sacredness of sex. The nuns considered masturbation sinful. At night, they insisted the boys' hands be kept in sight above their sheets. These harsh messages about sex evoked shame and confusion.

Neither of us had healed from these childhood experiences.

Matthew wanted to be a flower; Robert wanted us to be a family. Emily offered to be the child who would receive the love neither Robert nor I had known as children. I wanted to repair everything, to fix what was broken for my husband. I wanted to provide a loving family for Emily, Matthew, and myself. This was a tall order. I wanted honesty and loyalty to provide the foundation for my family and for my children. With all of our efforts and hopes, we were on a collision course.

The final blow to our marriage occurred when I discovered Robert was having an affair with his twenty-year-old secretary. I knew I could not, would not, live with lies and deceit that replicated what I had despised in my parents' marriage.

In retrospect, I see that our relationship was built on the flawed blueprints we both carried about love. Our marriage was made from good intentions and the debris of what Robert and I did and did not understand about love. Trauma repeats and repeats until it can be understood and healed.

The boy with the potted plant was the first child I ever loved, and I still love him today. My daughter, Emily, was born of this union. Both her father and I adore her. But our histories helped drive our marriage to its conclusion after seven years. In a way, he and I were both orphans seeking love, too ill equipped to create a loving union.

Chapter 26: HEY, DOC

The phone rings. Joel is calling ten minutes before his first appointment.

"I'm lost. I can't find your office." His anxiety is obvious.

"Where are you?"

"I just passed Howard and Western," he stutters.

"You are close," I say calmly, and give him turn-by-turn directions.

Despite getting lost, Joel is only five minutes late. "Sorry I'm late," he says. "Sorry, I am really sorry," he repeats. "Sorry."

Joel is less disheveled than I anticipated. His curly brown hair nicely frames his face; his forest green T-shirt is tucked into his blue jeans. But he has an urgency about him. He dives in, not wasting another minute.

"The reason I am here is that I don't want to fuck up my marriage. I really love my wife. I am a wreck. I am having panic attacks, and they keep getting worse." He sounds as though he is on fast forward and hardly breathes between statements. "I worry all the time that my wife is going to have an affair."

"Okay," I say to remind him that I am in the room and to try to connect with him. I wonder what triggered his ruminating.

"So, does your wife have a relationship with another man that is worrying you?"

"No, not really."

"When did the you begin to worry?"

"Right after we got married, I guess."

Joel is in his mid-thirties and a writer—which immediately causes me to feel a secret affinity with him. He has come to therapy because of his obsessive worries about his recent marriage. Sometimes his anxiety is so severe that he cannot write a word for days. Clearly, attachments are not a place of calm for Joel; they do not breed confidence. I wonder what life has taught him about relationships, loyalty, and safety.

"My parents separated when I was young," he tells me. "My father was a womanizer. He had affairs while he was married to my mom, which ruined their marriage. I might have forgiven him if he'd had an affair with someone he fell in love with, but I discovered that he'd had lots of affairs, like it was a damn hobby."

Joel hated this about his father.

"My uncle had affairs, too," he continues. "He even had an affair with one of my father's girlfriends."

These are the men in Joel's life, the male role models he does not want to emulate. I ask him to tell me about his wife: her interests, what they enjoy doing together.

"I have always encouraged my wife's love of music; she is a talented musician. Now she wants to go on the road with her band. They got a gig in New Orleans. She is totally excited."

His blue eyes glow with anxiety. He asks me, "Do you know what the music scene is *like*?"

Actually, despite our age difference, I do. I remember my twenties: the world of sex, drugs, and rock 'n' roll, late nights and cigarette smoke. I remember what we then called a time of freedom, crashing on someone's couch next to some guy you hardly knew.

I look at Joel. "Tell me what worries you about the music scene," I say, successfully squashing my ruminations about my past.

"Guys are going to want her. Opportunities!" He puts an exclamation mark at the end of the word. "The music scene is filled with sexual opportunities. Men are going to hit on her. She will be out late at night."

Joel wants to be a husband who supports his partner's dreams and aspirations, but he does not want her to go to New Orleans alone. He considers the idea of going along to protect his wife from the music world he imagines, filled with men and sex, seductive rhythms, and late nights with no regrets.

I am struck by how Joel pictures his wife as a victim of predatory men. He sees her as having no agency or responsibility of her own. Has he, I wonder, picked a partner—unknowingly, unconsciously—who has an affinity for affairs and one-night stands? Might she behave in a way that reminds him of his father and uncle, or that reinforces what he believes and fears about how love can go? Or does he believe that "opportunities" just have a life of their own?

Joel learned from watching his father that love can be destroyed by sexual desire, leaving a family in tatters. He is afraid of experiencing the chaos and traumas from his past in his new marriage.

"Have you talked to your wife about your fears?"

"I am afraid if I tell her how much I worry about this, I will drive her away."

"Would you consider telling her a little about the fears you have about her traveling with the band? You could share with her that your feelings of jealousy may be caused by what you witnessed in your family."

"That's a good idea," Joel replies. "Then she won't think that I think it is all about her or that I am some distrustful lunatic."

"You could also ask her to call you once a day, just to check in and let you know how the tour is going," I suggest. "That way, you can feel more connected and you won't have to imagine how she is spending her time."

Joel agrees that this is a good idea. "Thanks, Doc," he says. "That helped."

"I am not a doctor," I correct him. "You can call me Laurie, if you like."

He is not dissuaded. "See you next week, Doc."

———

The next week, Joel arrives five minutes late. "Hey, Doc. Sorry I'm late."

As is his style, he jumps in. "My wife and I have been getting along much better. In two weeks, she is going on another, even longer tour with her band. She told me not to worry about other guys hitting on her. She reassured me that she loves me and wants to be with me. As you suggested last week, I asked my wife if we could check in by phone every day while she is on the road. She agreed. I feel a little relief, but I still have a sense of dread. I feel like bad things will happen if I stop watching out for her."

Joel is on constant high alert. His body appears tense; his eyes are always darting around. Love, for Joel, is like a swirling cyclone that can potentially destroy everything in its path. Although he managed during his wife's first trip with her band, her reassurances do not quiet the force of his worries about his marriage and about her fidelity. I need to know more about what happened in Joel's past that prevents him from trusting his wife and believing in the sturdiness of his marriage.

"Joel, is this feeling of dread—this idea that if you stop watching out for someone, bad things will happen—something you have felt in the past, even before you met your wife?"

Joel pauses. "Yes, I guess I would say it's a feeling I had all the time after my father left when I was a kid."

Joel explains that after his father left his mother was very depressed. Alcohol became her steady companion. He constantly worried about her. "I got myself to school in the mornings. I ate a quick bowl of Cheerios or something. After school, I rushed home to check on my mom. I was always worried about her. Our house was such a mess. There were open cans of food, cigarette butts, and dirty clothes everywhere. I did the dishes, vacuumed the rugs, and scrubbed the sink so our apartment didn't smell so foul."

"How old were you?"

"I was nine when my father left."

"Joel, it seems that you didn't just lose your dad. In many ways you also lost a mother."

"I love my mom," he says forcefully.

I am sure Joel loves his mother. His zealous proclamation of his love for her strikes me as a boy who was disappointed in and abandoned by his father and needed someone to love, someone to love him. His mother was his only lifeline and essential to his tenuous self-worth. Even now, he can barely tolerate seeing her as having been injurious to him in any way.

"Did you feel like you had to keep an eye on your mom?" I ask.

"Yeah, she would be out late at night. I would look for her at the local bar. Sometimes I would wake up in the morning and find some strange man sleeping on our living room couch."

Betrayal blindness has allowed Joel to hold a prettier, less flawed picture of his mother. But I can see him beginning to acknowledge his mother's failure to provide what he needed as a child: love, nurturing, a stable home.

"Thanks for sharing that with me," I say. "I can see that it was not easy to do."

Because he is a writer, I ask Joel if he would be willing to record in his journal, without judgment, whatever feelings or memories he has about his mom.

"Okay, Doc," he agrees. "I can do that. As long as my writer's block doesn't get in the way."

The next week, Joel seems more agitated than usual. He sits on the edge of the couch. His left leg bounces up and down; the fingers on his right hand tap nervously on his other thigh.

"One thing I love and hate about writing is that it takes me places I might not otherwise go," he tells me. "It can turn my muddled musings into something with more clarity. It is where I have learned to tell naked truths."

I, too, know the power of writing to find the hidden truths.

"So I was writing, like you suggested," he says. "The first two days, nothing really came to me. Then, like in a daydream, I remembered this night with my mom."

"Can you tell me what you remembered?"

"One winter night, I walked home after going to my first dance at my high school. I remember it was snowy outside. I left my boots by the door. I said hi to my mom from the front door. I came inside and sat next to her on our living room couch. I could tell by her slurred speech that she had been seriously drinking." His leg bounces harder. "Then my mother puts both of her arms around my neck and she kisses me. Not a mom kind of kiss. She kisses me on the lips, and she puts her tongue in my mouth." Without taking a breath he adds, "I know she didn't know what she was doing. I hold my father responsible for her demise."

This is a difficult crossroads. To change the well-etched picture of the person you loved and treasured, the person you relied on for care, to include that this person also deeply hurt you, is a seismic psychological task. The fear of losing or damaging this primary, life-giving connection is agonizing.

"This experience with your mom sounds so disturbing," I say to Joel carefully, tenderly, knowing there is much at stake. "You were a young boy, just a teenager, which is such a vulnerable time. It was a time for you to discover your own sexuality, your identity. Teenagers want to be protected from their parents' sexuality, not assaulted by it."

Joel is quiet. Until now, I do not think he thought of himself during those years as being a boy. He was a boy passing as a man, trying to correct the sins of his father at great cost to himself.

Gender, too, plays tricks on our definitions and understandings of abuse. If this scene were reversed and instead a father kissed his daughter in this way, we would quickly identify it as abusive. Switch genders and our vision and clarity blur. Cultural gender misconceptions such as "mothers don't sexually abuse their sons" or "teenage boys can take care of themselves" or "boys see sex with older women as a conquest, not as abusive" all obscure the damage perpetrated on young boys. Although Joel would like to dismiss these moments with his mother and only think of her fondly, it is important he understand that they were instances of abuse and not minimize the disruption they caused to his sense of safety and security.

Over the next several weeks, Joel and I talk about his relationship with his mom, his feelings, and his unmet needs. He begins to see that she was not an innocent bystander to his father's betrayal of her and the family. He allows himself to be angry with his mother and sad about what he missed out on growing up. His obsessions and fears about his wife's potential infidelity begin to diminish. He becomes more productive. His writing life, he reports with pleasure, is back on track.

But then, several weeks later, Joel calls me on the phone. "Hi, Doc. Can I make an appointment to see you on Monday?"

I now realize that when Joel calls me "Doc," he is trying to protect himself from me, a woman who is supposed to care about him, by defining my role. He wants to be sure that the boundaries between us are not blurred.

On Monday, his agitation is back.

"I am obsessing again about my wife having an affair," he tells me. "My fear plays on loop in my head. My worries quieted down for a while, and I hoped that I was cured. But she is leaving on a tour next week with the guys in her band. I know that guys will want her."

Joel still imagines his wife as an innocent bystander. As if affairs happen to people rather than because people make choices. Although we have explored many difficult aspects of his past, Joel is still operating based on beliefs about love he learned as a child.

I ask him if he would be willing to visualize something.

"I'm game, Doc, if you think it will help."

"Imagine you are surrounded by beautiful women," I say. "They all think that you are an amazing writer. Your wife is nowhere to be found. There are opportunities to be with these women, to have sex with them. What are you thinking?"

"Um . . . I am excited and a little afraid." His right knee bounces up and down.

I ask him if he will stay with the fantasy. He nods. So I ask him to imagine what happens next.

"I don't do anything."

"What are you thinking now?" I inquire.

His eyes are still closed. "I am thinking, I am married. I am committed to my wife. I don't want to have sex with anyone else."

"Now," I ask, "can you notice what you are feeling?"

A tear appears on his cheek. "Calm," he says.

Joel's parents were reckless in love and reckless with their sexuality. This led him to believe that everyone is powerless before the forces of love and sexual desire.

"I can make a choice," he says. "My parents made choices, bad ones. I know that sounds silly, but I am not sure I knew that they had these choices." His face is visibly more relaxed. "So," he says, "no matter what I feel, or what opportunities there might be, I have a choice and so does my wife."

Joel is coming to know a new definition of love, a definition that pairs feelings and passion with commitment and responsibility. Joel has become the kind of man he hoped he would be, the kind of man he wished he had known as a boy.

As Joel leaves my office, for the first time without hesitation, his eyes meet mine. He shakes my hand and says, "Thanks, Laurie."

PART 3

"We ask too much of love—
but surprisingly love often delivers."
—Richard Todd

Chapter 27: **TRUST**

Abusive relationships lack mutuality; they honor only one person's needs, desires, or goals. Empathic concern for the other person is conspicuously absent. Mutuality is the quality I hope my clients will come to know and recognize in relationships; relationships in which both people can grow, where no one is silenced.

Feminist therapists have written extensively about the importance of mutuality in the therapeutic relationship. Mutuality means both people in the relationship are affected by the work. Many therapists acknowledge being moved and inspired by their clients' courage and resilience. These therapists strive to be authentic and transparent in their emotional connection with their clients. How lovely and affirming it sounds—but there is a messier side of mutuality, one that therapists seldom acknowledge.

Many well-meaning therapists honor the premise of mutuality but prefer that vulnerability remain on the client's side of the room. But true mutuality requires that the therapist be willing to be ripped open on occasion, to sometimes feel humiliated, baffled, and horrified.

Unspoken and unprocessed traumas from the past insist on being known. They are enacted between the client and therapist.

These enactments can be disruptive and destructive. Even the most aware and experienced therapist can fall down the rabbit hole. Like the powerful undertow of the ocean, traumatic enactments deserve respect, awe, and extreme caution.

———

It's a beautiful, warm spring day, and I'm eagerly anticipating the upcoming appointment with Elizabeth. I am still careful not to disrupt the consistency and structure of her therapy sessions. I warned her three weeks before I painted my office a different color so as to not alarm her.

But today, I can't avoid surprising her. I have never asked her for anything before, certainly not anything that I desired. I hope she will be honored, as my other clients have been. It is only a paragraph in an eighteen-page article. If it's a problem, she can just say no. I asked her to reserve an extra few minutes after our session today to talk. I do not want my agenda to interfere with the time designated for her therapy.

Elizabeth is a different person now than she was when she began therapy. I am proud of the work we have done together. I think about last week, when Elizabeth turned tenderly toward me to wave good-bye as she walked down the hall from my office after our session. I know there is more work ahead of us, but today I am basking in the sunlight and in the warmth of the relationship Elizabeth and I have miraculously formed.

Elizabeth arrives wearing a flowered dress with an empire waist; she has only recently begun wearing clothing that highlights her shapely body. She, too, seems energized by the possibilities of spring. Her new glasses fit nicely on her face, replacing the oversized black frames she used to wear. These changes are all signs of how far she has come.

The article I'm planning to submit to a professional journal was difficult for me to write. I am not well suited to the constraints of professional journals. The last time I submitted an article, the editor told me it was too poetic. I was secretly thrilled.

When our session ends, I remind Elizabeth that we reserved some extra time so I could talk to her. I am ready to pose my question.

I sip my lukewarm tea. I suddenly feel exposed and vulnerable sharing a piece of my professional life with Elizabeth—similar to how she once felt sharing her successes with me. I am anxious about putting a toe outside the honored therapist/client framework I prudently protect. I take a deep breath.

"Elizabeth, I am working on an article for a journal. I so value the work we do together. I have learned so much from you. I was hoping I could use an example from our work in the article. Of course, I will change your name and any details that would interfere with confidentiality."

As the last word rolls off my tongue, I see Elizabeth's expression change. Her eyes tell a story of fear.

"What are you thinking?" I ask.

"I feel like I have to say yes to you," she says. "I have to please you."

I am disturbed by her response. "I understand that you may feel compelled to say yes, but I really don't want you to agree to something if it doesn't feel right to you."

"I am afraid if I say no, you will be very mad at me," Elizabeth says.

"I will not be mad. Maybe a little disappointed, but certainly not mad."

"I cannot say no to you," she declares as if it is an immutable fact.

I quickly attempt to reassure her again. "I will not be mad if you say no. My greater investment is in your well-being and in our relationship. That is more important to me than permission to use an example of our work for an article."

Elizabeth says, "I know I have to say yes. And if I say yes to you, I will go home and hurt myself."

Elizabeth believes she only has two choices: say yes and betray herself or say no and destroy our connection. I attempt to empathize with her feelings.

"What a terrible bind," I say. "You feel that either you comply and hate yourself, or say no and then believe you are at risk of destroying our relationship."

Elizabeth does not respond. Her distress only increases, and she stares at the floor. I have lost her, lost our connection. She is mute. She stands up and walks out of my office.

I am stunned by the intensity of her reaction. I am horrified that there is nothing I can do to shift what is unraveling in front of me.

This is the first time the ghosts from Elizabeth's traumatic past have invaded our relationship. They are haunting us, distorting reality and twisting what was good between us. I feel a burning sensation in my abdomen, a visceral sense of the crushing weight of the life-threatening double bind created by her father's abuse. I can taste the horror she experienced as a child with an abuser she needed to love. I feel helpless to reconnect and reassure her.

———————

Later, I reflect on what happened, and I can see we were in a traumatic reenactment. Elizabeth was reliving the excruciating bind of an abused child. She wanted to please her perpetrator, the person she was dependent upon and who was supposed to love and protect her, but when she pleased him, she felt complicit in her abuse. And the aftermath was cascading self-hatred and shame. Now she is experiencing the traumatic bind of her abusive past as if it is happening in the present. She learned that those who love you want to control and destroy you. As a child, she was taught how to charm and soothe the ego of her caretaker, the man who loved, tortured, and abused her. Her untold story is appearing between us.

I am eager to talk to Elizabeth to decode with her the traumatic reenactment we experienced. I hope this will be an opportunity for us to explore and deepen our understanding of the horrors of her past; in doing so, I believe we can further understand and transform her fear of intimate relationships.

———

Elizabeth calls and leaves me a message saying that she does not think she can return to therapy. "I don't think that I can ever trust you again," she says between sobs.

I am devastated. In one moment, I have become the perpetrator, the violator, the destroyer; the deep trust we built over ten years has vanished.

These are difficult moments for any therapist. We who are on the side of our clients' healing are challenged to tolerate the unflattering pictures of ourselves that our clients sometimes hold. In these moments, some therapists withdraw or subtly retaliate. I can imagine this. I could say, "Okay. Good luck; it has been nice working with you for ten years," feigning the cruelty of indifference. But I am not indifferent. I want to repair what has broken.

I call Elizabeth back. She picks up.

"Hi, Elizabeth."

"Hi."

"I am really sorry you are in so much pain. I think if you come in to talk, we can figure out together what happened between us yesterday. I thought you were ready to have this kind of conversation. I did not realize the distress it would cause you."

I don't remember exactly what else I say, but whatever it is, it makes things worse.

Elizabeth is now even more furious. "I am not coming back to therapy until you apologize for all the damage you have caused."

"I hope you come in for your session tomorrow," I say in a matter-of-fact tone.

Elizabeth reiterates, "I am not coming back until you apologize for what you did. Bye."

I am seething. I feel unjustly blamed, accused, and punished for the crimes of her past. Doesn't she understand the value of our relationship and the trust we have painstakingly built? How did I end up fully clothed in the garments of her abusers?

Elizabeth later complains that my tone lacked warmth and that I was distant and clinical. I imagine she was right.

After missing one week, Elizabeth agrees to come in for a session. I raise the question of understanding what occurred between us. I ask if we can explore what it can tell us about her past that might be meaningful. I explain how it is not unusual for survivors of trauma to reenact with their therapists aspects of their past.

"I will not talk about my past with you," she says. "I only want to talk about your apology."

I am mad, defensive. I have been stripped of my therapeutic access to the parts of Elizabeth that are able to reflect. I feel like a criminal on trial. I do not know what crime I have committed or what more I can apologize for. I tell her that the question of the article is off the table. I promise that I will not consider writing about her unless she suggests otherwise in the future.

"You were wrong to decide I was ready for the conversation about the article rather than ask me," Elizabeth explains.

"I am sorry. You are right. I should not have assumed that you were ready for that conversation. I wish I had asked you first rather than assumed."

The word "ready" stays with me. My mind wanders to the Christmas when her father spoke the same words. He said he thought she was "ready," which meant she was ready for his sexual conquest. I understand that interpretation can be a way that a therapist exerts power, so I refrain. But the connection stays with me, and I wonder if that is what is fueling the intensity of her feelings and distress.

———

During our next session, I begin by asking Elizabeth, "What would you like to talk about?"

She says my question is cold and minimizes the disaster that occurred between us.

I think about the research done by Constance Dalenberg, PhD, who discovered that trauma survivors' greatest fear is that they will trigger their therapists' withdrawal. For these clients, Dalenberg found, a cold and distant response from their therapist actually increases their sense of humiliation and shame.

I realize that I am guilty as charged. It was not what I said or didn't say that devastated Elizabeth; rather, it was my defensiveness, my coldness, and my emotional withdrawal. I believe I expressed my anger more through distancing than through open hostility, which further exacerbated Elizabeth's suffering.

Elizabeth responds to my detached professional demeanor. "I will not talk to you about my past," she reiterates. "You no longer have the right to have that kind of access to me."

The next day, she calls me to tell me that she wants to consult with other therapists to determine if it is safe for her to continue to work with me.

"I think we can find a way to work this out," I tell her. "You certainly have the right to speak to whoever you want."

I feel threatened by her desire to consult with others. One of the disadvantages of being a therapist who is known and trusted in the larger community is that Elizabeth will likely consult with other professionals who are my colleagues or therapists I have mentored or trained. I wonder if she intends to share the list of crimes I committed with others who know and respect me; it seems she is looking for a way to get an upper hand in a battle, rather than seeking a way to repair our relationship. During the next weeks, she speaks with the editor of a journal in my field, as well as three other therapists who know me well.

It is easier to see the wounded parts of our clients and ignore the parts of them that can be hurtful to others or to us. I decide that instead of hiding my fears of humiliation the next time I see her, I will tell her what I am thinking, and I do.

"Elizabeth, you know that I am professionally visible in my field," I tell her during our next session. "This actually gives you power to publically humiliate me and to do harm to my reputation. I don't know if that is something you want to do, but I want to acknowledge the possibility and the power you hold."

"Oh, I would never do that," she says.

I am distraught and realize I need help. I call a colleague in Connecticut who writes extensively about the impact of trauma work on therapists. Like me, she also trains therapists in working with trauma. I am sure she understands the inevitable twists of traumatic reenactments. I know she can hold the complexity of my feelings without doubting my investment in the well-being of my client.

I tell her about what had happened with Elizabeth. I say I am furious, that I feel misunderstood and on trial for crimes I did not commit. She listens attentively, and kindly acknowledges the important work that I have done with Elizabeth and her respect for my work and for me.

I take a deep breath, exhaling my hurt and sense of being wronged. Underneath is my deep attachment to Elizabeth and sadness about the loss of the trust that we've worked so hard to establish. I reflect on how wounded I feel. I also acknowledge my own past of disrupted and damaged attachments.

My colleague reminds me that Elizabeth is deeply traumatized, frightened, and unable to reflect on what is happening between us. Her entire central nervous system is on high alert; her trust is still too fragile. It is my job to soothe her and provide a safe place for her, free from my anger.

My colleague is, of course, correct.

I am relieved to have someone to talk to who listens, empathizes with my distress, and helps me think about how to get my work with Elizabeth back on track. My anger dissipates.

———

I have not seen Elizabeth for three weeks. I miss her, and I'm anxious. When she arrives, she looks tentative, hurt, and frightened.

"Thank you for coming," I say sincerely. "I know it must be really difficult."

"It is really hard," she affirms. "I don't feel safe with you."

"I understand that. We will have to go slow and work on rebuilding trust."

Elizabeth nods. "I don't want to talk about my past with you; that is still out of bounds."

"That makes sense to me. Those things are very precious and intimate—something you would share with someone you deeply trust, not someone you feel deeply wounded by."

I can see her shoulders relax. But she is not ready to talk. I ask her if she wants to draw with me.

She nods.

We sit, side by side, with paper and crayons. I make a smile on one side of the paper. With several different colored crayons I write, "I am glad to see you."

A brief smile appears on her face. In blue and red crayons, she writes, "I Missed You. Are You Really Back? Are You Safe?"

I take a green crayon and print next to her question. "I Am Sorry I Hurt You. It May Take Time to Feel Safe with Me Again. I Think You Got Really Scared."

She nods yes.

Repair has truly begun.

———

Slowly, over many weeks, Elizabeth begins to share more. She tells me how pleased she is that she and her new friend are riding bikes together on the lakeshore path on Saturdays.

I smile and tell her how wonderful it is that they are enjoying each other.

I am softer. My edginess evaporates.

Over time, we cautiously speak about what had transpired between us. Elizabeth tells me that when I mentioned that I would be disappointed if she did not give me permission to use an example from our work for my article, she felt terrified.

"Maybe you were disappointed with me?" I suggest. "Sharing disappointments is not dangerous. Actually, it can actually build and deepen trust."

The corners of her mouth turn upward, just a bit, in a hesitant smile. "I was disappointed in you," she says.

"I bet you were."

Months pass, and slowly our relationship returns to a more open, trusting one. The fight or flight response of the trauma passes. As we repair what was broken, she can again reflect.

"The women in my family had such impoverished stories about what love requires," she says. "If you did not comply with what someone wanted you to do or be, you faced the threat of abandonment. Power is the language of love in my family. I never knew about the kind of relationships where someone really cares about you, where you can work through a conflict without destroying each other. It's funny, but having worked through this with you makes me feel more able to have a good relationship. I don't think I will trust anyone until we have our first fight and successfully work it through."

I am relieved and pleased, and so is she.

"I think this was hard on you, too," she says.

A tear slips down my cheek. "Yes, it was hard," I tell her. "But sometimes, hard is part of being committed to someone you treasure."

Two years later, Elizabeth says, "I have something I want to say to you."

"What is it?" I ask.

"I have decided that it is okay with me if you want to write about me. Please use the name Elizabeth if you do."

I nod. I try not to reveal the mixture of joy, relief, and residual trepidation I feel.

This is a momentous act of trust. Elizabeth is not making this offer because she feels threatened or obligated to comply. Nothing is being extracted from her.

I believe it is an act of love. The kind of love where there are not winners and losers, where connection and individual choice are no longer at odds.

Chapter 28: BREAK AND REPAIR

I t is not the perfect parent who creates secure and resilient children; it is the good-enough parent, the parent who protects children from the big breaks that would frighten and terrify them but allows and embraces the constant flow of smaller breaks and repairs. As Carol Gilligan eloquently writes in her book, *Birth of Pleasure*, "It is the cycles of break and repair that build the vocabulary of love and trust."

Being a good-enough parent is a dance, not a formula that guarantees success. "Attunement," some call it. It's a matter of noticing how the child feels, comforting the child, delighting in the child, accepting the child, and recognizing that neither the child, nor life, nor the parent is perfect. The good-enough parent makes mistakes, apologizes to the child, and accepts the child's apologies, modeling relationships built on trust and mutuality. When others hurt the child's feelings, the good-enough parent is there for support. When the child causes harm, the good-enough parent helps the child make amends. Break and repair is the foundation for a solid sense of self and a connection to others. It's the foundation for love.

Shame is the opposite. It is the experience of injury with no repair. When a child's vulnerability and needs are met with rejection, indifference, or ridicule, the child experiences word-less shame.

Shame has a narrative. It is a story of a defective self, unworthy of love or tenderness. Clients who share this narrative of shame use the words "unlovable," "defective," "disgusting," "repulsive," and "not quite human" to describe how they feel about themselves.

Shame stories are about self-blame. They lack compassion for the victim and accountability for the abuser. Shame has no context; it is blind to the trauma that has occurred and its impact. Shame doesn't reflect and has no room for shades of grey; everything is black and white. Shame is the dreadful outcome of interpersonal trauma. It is the failure of love and the absence of repair.

For my clients, abuse is not a single incident. It is a sustained experience of breaks without repair. To quiet shame, to create a different narrative devoid of stories of shame, we must create new experiences of nurturing relationships.

Break and repair is the language of love. It's so simple, yet so difficult.

Repair requires that an injured person reach out, trusting they will not be met with indifference or ridicule. This is more than difficult. Most survivors of abuse haven't experienced gestures of repair in their previous relationships. "No. Never. I will not. I cannot. I won't." These are not the words of a resistant client but the protective efforts of a traumatized person protecting the shreds of their dignity.

For trauma therapists to succeed, we must become masters of repair. It is a difficult process, and we make mistakes along the way.

Therapists are shy to acknowledge their failures. We, too, are afraid of ridicule, of not looking good in the eyes of our peers or supervisors. Most of the literature about therapy features moments of revelation; there is little written about therapeutic mistakes. But mistakes are unavoidable for the trauma therapist, and our reluctance to acknowledge our errors can interfere with our ability to create new relational experiences with our clients. Accountability is essential for healthy relationships and for repairs. Lack of accountability is endemic in the lives of abused children, and it breeds blame and shame, not connection and repair. Our job is to create a new experience of a relationship based on accountability and compassion. This requires that we reflect on the impact we have on our clients and stay mindful of the impact our clients have on us.

Our mistakes don't frighten our clients. What happens next is what matters. If a client points out a mistake or failure on our part, do we react defensively? Do we subtly shift the blame to them with an interpretation? Do we make the artless therapist mistake and respond with a nod of our head and say nothing?

Traumatized clients report that their greatest fear is that they will evoke uncomfortable feelings in their therapist, and she or he will respond by shaming them or distancing from them. We do this even though we know we shouldn't. When I am overwhelmed or frightened, or when I feel shamed by a client, my first response is to get quiet, shut down, and emotionally abandon them. My lack of response can feel like indifference and mortify my client.

Moments of break and repair are fraught; they test our relationships. Can we remain undiminished by the demands or discomfort of one other? Can we reflect on what went wrong between us? Can our conflicts be about difference rather than insistence on compliance? Can we use our voices to deepen our knowledge and regard for each other rather than cause further injuries?

After years of working with Jessica, I receive this handwritten note one day:

Dear Laurie,
Since we probably won't talk today, I thought I would write
a brief note about yesterday. You really did not mention
anything about your week off, except for not being there
for Group on Dec. 30. This is unusual for you. So far, your
habit has been to hand me a sticky paper with your out-of-
office dates and reiterate out loud.

You are too responsible of a person to merely have
forgotten to tell me. Also, I think you know very well
that for most people, to screw up 4 hours of their day
has multiple repercussions involving multiple people. So,
I am wondering about your reaction and what is going
on with you. I don't know how you handle that, but that
seems to be at the heart of this matter.
Jessica

I respond:

Dear Jessica,
I would like to respond to your note. Yes, it is a big
deal to mess with four hours of a person's day, and my
response did not adequately acknowledge the negative
impact my behavior had on you. I was truly stunned
that I would have overlooked telling you about my week
off. I so treasure our relationship and the work we
do together. I am truly sorry.

It is my responsibility to stay aware of my
reactions and to manage them responsibly. At this
moment, I do not think my behavior was a reflection
on anything about our relationship. Maybe more a
reflection of bigger issues that have to do with my work. I
will think more about it and share with you my thoughts
and reflections when we talk.

Ironically, I am pleased that you are holding me accountable. It shows so much growth on your part and a shift in your beliefs about what you can and should expect from people who care about you.

I think you are wonderful. How about we talk at 2 P.M. tomorrow? Let me know what number to call you at.
With Care, Laurie

Within hours I receive:

Dear Laurie,
Ok, I feel that your response is terrific and I am reassured that you will reflect personally on whatever bigger issues may be at hand. That is what I really wanted to know you would do.

We don't have to talk tomorrow. Just enjoy the coming of the New Year. We can talk at our next scheduled time, Monday, Jan. 4th at 2, unless you tell me otherwise. I, too, so treasure our relationship and the work we do together.
Happy New Year, Laurie—
Warmly, Jessica.

A simple moment of break and repair, where what happened between us is in stark contrast to the denial and cruelty Jessica has known in the past. It was unthinkable for Jessica to express her distress about anything her parents did or failed to do. Fear and threat silenced her. Conflict was dangerous, trust was nonexistent, and empathy or compassion for the impact others had on her was unimaginable.

These small moments, coupled with many other small and bigger moments, are where the lessons of love reside. Repairs are hard-won. But they change everything.

Chapter 29: **BLACK AND BLUE**

Sara waves good-bye to her father from the back window of her mother's decrepit car. Smoke rises from beneath the car. Her mother has finally gathered the courage to leave her abusive husband. With little money and few possessions, they drive out of town toward the hills. In the next town, her uncle has an apartment above his restaurant. He has agreed to allow five-year-old Sara and her mother to live above his restaurant in exchange for her mother's work as a waitress.

The smells of bacon and fried eggs greet them in the early morning. Sara and her mother are relieved to be away from the violence, and to be together.

Things go well at first, but not for long. The uncle frightens the little girl, as he once frightened her mother when he sexually abused her when she was a child. He is not a safe person.

Sara's mother begins to drink at night and then in the mornings, too. She sleeps too much. Sometimes she does not go to work and is unable to clean the house or wash the dishes. Sara eats her dinner out of an empty flowerpot.

———

Sara is in her mid-twenties when we first meet. She is tall and slender, with a chiseled nose and large blue eyes. She is gifted with language; her words are like poetry.

Sara says she is grateful to have found me. She has searched for someone she can talk to about her life and about sexual abuse. She thinks my experience and reputation uniquely qualify me to help her. However, as therapy proceeds, she is often disappointed, and she is not shy about letting me know. She often finds my observations off, my caring too shallow, and my responses to her difficulties and experiences lacking the right intensity.

To provide healing we must be accountable when we fail or inadvertently injure our clients. We must be willing to be humbled again and again, and to make repairs when necessary.

One day in my office, Sara tells me about an experience when she was fifteen. She spares no details about when she was raped by three older boys. I am horrified by the gruesome details and by the brutality of the gang rape. I am overwhelmed.

The therapist and client share some common challenges. We both need to know and don't want to know about these moments when heartlessness, cruelty, and brutality demolish a young girl's body and soul. Sara needs a compassionate witness who is alive and present, but in this moment I am speechless and momentarily traumatized. I, too, can be devastated in my role as witness to the traumas that my clients have endured. Some call this a secondary or vicarious trauma. It is not a flaw; it is just a normal human consequence of confronting human atrocities.

During our next session, Sara tells me she felt like I was not empathetic when she described the sexual assault.

I attempt to explain what happened. "Last week, when you described the gang rape, I felt devastated and shocked," I tell her. "When I care about someone and hear about how they have been viciously and cruelly assaulted, words temporarily escape me. I am so sorry you felt so alone at a time you so needed to know I cared about you and about what happened to you."

I do something radically different from what others in Sara's life have done: I acknowledge the impact of my behavior on her. I have disappointed her and I have inadvertently injured someone I care about.

Sara nods. She understands this state of shock and the loss of language that accompanies traumatic events.

I ask Sara if it would be helpful if I write my feelings down on paper as they become clear to me after difficult sessions. "I can then share my feelings with you the next time we meet."

"Oh yes," she says. "That would be great."

Sara has not known adults who take responsibility when they fail her. Apologies, love paired with responsibility and accountability, were absent in the many abusive relationships she has known. She is pleased and surprised that I have apologized and offered a way of fixing the breech between us.

Months later, she alerts me to another concern about our relationship.

"I am not sure I am safe here," Sara begins. "After our last session, when you said good-bye, I saw romance in your eyes."

I am stunned. I quickly scan my feelings. Romance? No. Not even a hint of it. What I notice are maternal feelings. Tenderness. But I do not have any romantic or sexual feelings.

The confusion between affection and sexual feelings is one of the lasting scars from childhood sexual abuse. Fear, arousal, affection, and rage mingle together. A child lacks words to distinguish one from the other. The wires get crossed, and the result is that eroticism and nurturing become confused.

Sara has shown me what she learned from her ongoing traumatic experiences, where adults who were supposed to care for and protect her instead sexualized and abused her.

"I do not have romantic feelings for you," I reassure her. "I do cherish you and the work we do together."

One hot, muggy summer day, we have another rupture. Sara enters my office and tugs the door closed. The humidity has caused the wooden door to swell to the point that it will not shut tightly. I assure Sara that her safety will not be compromised with the door so slightly ajar, but she is not soothed. She insists that her privacy is being violated. She believes I am not protecting her adequately.

Sara does not see things in shades of grey. When she experiences even a slight or imagined betrayal, her body goes into a full trauma response, as if the crimes of her childhood are recurring in the moment. She has not learned to soothe herself and recognize the difference between minor and major injuries in relationships. To Sara, all mistakes evoke the same feelings of past betrayals.

When people experience pervasive abuse, neglect, and the absence of safety, their brains are wired to survive. They are on high alert; they sense danger is always lurking. Stress hormones flood their bodies, even in the absence of an actual assault. A perceived betrayal triggers this response. Sara's brain is finely tuned to perceive and react to fear and abandonment. She is stuck in the trauma and has difficulty incorporating new information and experiences. It is my job—our job—to literally change the brain's response and activate new patterns.

I ask Sara to breathe and to notice what she is feeling in her body.

"I feel frightened and mad," she replies.

I ask her if she can look around the room and tell me what she sees. By using her senses, I am helping to ground her in the present. She describes the tapestry on the wall: the grey, black, and cream-colored threads.

I ask her what she feels now. "Calm," she says. "I am not in any danger."

I explain to Sara that it is important for her to notice when she is truly in danger and when she is not. "There are small black-

and-blue marks in all relationships," I tell her. "We all make small mistakes in our close relationships. When we are wrong, we can apologize. Even the best relationships are imperfect." Sara's face softens; this is news to her. She relaxes and her anger dissipates. We have interrupted the pattern of her hardwired over-response to fear for the moment, but until she develops the capacity to reflect and discern, she will fall back into this pattern again and again. This is what we must work on in therapy; she needs new interactions and experiences inside and outside of our relationships to create neural pathways to replace the old ones. This is the miracle of neuroplasticity. The brain can be rewired for healthier and more effective responses. But it will take time and numerous repetitions.

With her knack for the lyrical, Sara says, "You are my Annie Sullivan when it comes to relationships. You keep putting my hand under the water and saying W – A – T – E – R, water, water, water. I think I get it."

Chapter 30: GOOD-BYE

The snow on the winding path to Haimowoods melted, the apple trees bloomed, and the hot summer sun turned the dirt path to dust. Then the trees burst into brilliant oranges and reds. Soon snow covered the path again. I returned weekly for ten years.

I was learning from Natalie as a therapist. My skills improved, my insights deepened, and I eagerly brought all of this back to my own practice, where I steadily gained confidence and dexterity. But she was far more than a mentor to me; she was also my anchor, and I came to depend on our weekly sessions to keep myself grounded as I grew emotional parts of myself that had been stunted from a family full of secrets, lies, and absences.

I had a crush on Natalie. Others might call my infatuation with my therapist a sign of transference—a projection of my longings for a mother who loved me. But I felt like I was unraveling. I had carefully created the persona of a self-reliant, rough-and-tumble girl in business for herself. I had fired my mother at a young age. I simply thought that if my mother didn't care about me, I wouldn't care about her, either. I thought, *Who needs a mother anyway?* This carefully constructed self, in which I had successfully buried all my longings, was shifting under my feet.

Secretly, I longed for a woman like Natalie, one whom I could admire and who could teach, guide, and nurture me—show me how to become a woman with dignity. Natalie was smart and effective. Her life was brimming with purpose. She was disciplined in her work, and she was generous with her heart. In her presence, I was a raw mess of yearnings.

The problem was, I did not embrace my longings. Quite the contrary. I was not what you would call an endearing client. In the Monday therapy group, I was angry and distrustful; I cried a lot for no apparent reason. During and after group sessions, I often had a headache and panic prickled my arms and slid down to my hands. I did not understand my feelings. But Natalie was steady and attentive.

My memory of what Natalie and I spoke about is spotty at best. A cacophony of grief and longing mixed with a fragile sense of self emerged from a place within me that I had never known. I panicked when she left the room at the end of each session. Without intending to, I had found someone who cared about me, who accepted me. It was as though she had cracked open my carefully guarded veneer and inside was my younger self, devastated by the distance and absence of my own mother. I had little control over this process at first, and I was also reluctant to go through it. Everything I had done to survive my mother's absence was falling away; I felt completely off balance. But I continued to come for sessions with Natalie, week after week, month and month. Slowly, gradually, I began to be able to talk about my losses and identify my feelings. My headaches subsided, and I grew to trust her. My panic was replaced with pleasurable anticipation of being in her company.

One day, I turned to Natalie to ask her a question I had never dared to ask before.

"Do you really like me?"

Without a pause, without any sign of hesitation, she answered. "Do I like you? I love you."

Natalie, the consummate professional—insightful, disciplined, compassionate, and caring—had said she loved me. Unbelievable. Shocking. Amazing.

This extraordinary moment startled and changed me. My secret self—the one I concealed from others and from myself, the child within me who longed for love, who had longed for her mother's love—could no longer hide or feign indifference.

That night, in the privacy of my apartment, I curled up on the mattress on the floor in my makeshift living room, and an inarticulate sound slowly rose from somewhere inside me. It gradually intensified into the piercing sobs of a young child—a sound so primitive, so real, and so undeniable. This undignified mixture of tears, drool, and snot soaked my bed. After some hours in the stillness of the night, I finally drifted off to sleep.

Natalie, the woman I most admired, cared about me. My pervasive insecurity, anxiety, and self-doubt were fading. My fragments were knitting together into a more vibrant self. I felt loved, and that mattered. I felt more secure in myself, more generous and more compassionate. Natalie gave me a new roadmap, one that guided me to become a woman with purpose and integrity. Now I knew an amazing woman I could love and emulate.

Four years later, I returned to Natalie's Victorian house for the last time. The potbelly stove in the foyer radiated warmth. Smells from the kitchen filled the house. The dining room table held the usual things that Natalie provided for gatherings of beloved friends, colleagues, and students: homemade breads, vegetables and dips, and a large casserole. I filled my plate and walked into the adjoining living room, where Natalie was receiving her students and colleagues. But this time, she struggled for words. The curse of a degenerative neurological condition was robbing her of her ability to speak coherently.

I could not imagine a world without her to guide me. After most of the other guests left, I sat next to her, our fingers entwined. She smiled. Talking was difficult, but she insisted on trying. I leaned close. Slowly, deliberately, she said, "I . . . am . . . so proud . . . of you."

I was not as brave as she was. Tears flooded my eyes. Natalie kissed me on my cheek. I did not want to say good-bye. I couldn't.

Two years later, I visited Natalie and Morris in Oakland, California, where they had moved to be close to family. I was afraid that when I looked into Natalie's eyes, her brilliance would be extinguished and I would be overcome with grief. I walked slowly, deliberately, to the door of their small cottage, attempting to steady my breathing. I was struck by the contrast between their new home and the Victorian house, with its oversized door and big living room that I had visited so often. By the steps, a small vegetable garden overflowed with large red tomatoes.

I ascended the three wooden stairs to the porch where Natalie sat on a swing. Morris had warned me that she might not recognize me. We looked at each other. I hugged her; she welcomed the warmth of my body close to hers. I saw a tear in her eye. Morris was stunned.

I sat in the wrought iron chair next to Natalie and took her hand in mine. The California sun warmed my back I was happy, very happy, to be with her again. I was not overcome with grief. I felt tender and reassured by the depth of love I felt with her and for her.

This was the last time I saw Natalie, the woman who taught me about purpose, integrity, and the capacity to love. She remains my reference point, the standard to which I aspire.

Chapter 31: THE WOMEN IN MY LIFE

My father and Annie liked each other. Their relationship was different from his relationship with my mother. Unlike my mother, Annie wallpapered the bathrooms and painted the living room herself. She learned to make tightly woven Nantucket baskets, to do calligraphy, and to paint watercolors of Nantucket beaches. Annie went on fishing trips with my father. Unlike my mother, she was happy in blue jeans and a waterproof parka and was not afraid to bait her own hook.

My father no longer needed me as an ally. However, some things did not change.

Once when I visited them in Nantucket, their retirement paradise, afternoon light flooded their living room. We sat on nubby white couches with embroidered pillows. The condensation from their scotch glasses dripped onto plastic coasters. My father looked at me and then at Annie. He smiled and said, "I can't figure out which one of you I want to sleep with tonight."

Annie said nothing. I was dazed. Why was I the object of these flirtations? And why was Annie not outraged? Like my mother, she remained impassive as my father made inappropriate sexual comments about me. Was it a magic trick? Abracadabra, with a sleight of hand, you will only see what you want to see—certainly not the fact that this man is coming on to his daughter—and ignore everything else.

Did I mishear, I wondered? Or was this a syndrome, a sexual Tourette's of sorts, that no one wanted to acknowledge? When I was younger, I learned to go blank when my father spoke to me like that. Sometimes I remembered what he said, but often I did not. I could feel and not feel the pervasive erotic charge in the daylight hours. Was this just what men who are "sweet and lovable" get to do?

Why did my mother not fight for me? Why did she not insist that my father treat me as their daughter and not see me as her competitor? Why did these women turn their backs on their daughter? Why did I become speechless?

Later, one winter when Emily was eleven years old, we went to visit my father and Annie in Florida. Emily was excited about seeing her grandparents. They greeted us with smiles, Coca-Cola, iced tea, and homemade cookies. It was hot, and Emily couldn't wait to jump into their pool.

Emily squeezed into her one-piece, flowered bathing suit. Her joy and anticipation of the water erased her self-consciousness about her body, which was beginning to show signs of a woman's shape. Emily reached the edge of the pool and jumped in. Her smile sparkled through the drops of water that splashed upwards toward her face. I loved watching her joyous abandon.

After splashing around in the pool for more than an hour, Emily dried off and joined us in the kitchen for lunch. We ate turkey and roast beef sandwiches on rye bread from the local deli—my father's favorites, I fondly remembered from my childhood. Emily remained at the kitchen table with a deck of cards, playing solitaire, as I cleared the table and washed the dishes.

Emily looked up at her grandfather, who was sitting across from her. "Grandpa, do you want to play gin rummy with me?"

"Not really," he replied. "I would much rather make mad, passionate love to you."

In that moment, my dissociation lifted and my maternal strings catapulted me out of my father's trance. I did not wonder, as I had in the past, if I had misheard my father. Blood rose to my face; my complexion turned bright red. I stared into my father's baby blue eyes and, with fire in my voice, I said, "Do not ever speak to my daughter like that again." I paused, then added, "Or this will be the last time you ever see your granddaughter."

My father was silent. He pretended, as he always had, that this encounter was not happening. But I knew what I'd heard; my reality did not waver. My daughter would not be the recipient of his obscene displays.

That day, at my father's kitchen table, I challenged the legacy of women in my family who'd turned away from their daughters and refused to notice when they were injured.

My father never spoke to my daughter inappropriately again.

Chapter 32: THE DATE

It is easy to identify the footprints of trauma. They leave marks on psyches, they wreak havoc on close relationships, and they destroy dreams. Calm is replaced with alarm, love with suspicion. But there are also the footprints of repair and healing, that are softer, less obvious than the roar of trauma.

Hours before Group, Wendy leaves me a phone message: "I hope you are sitting down. Are you ready for a real shocker? I had a date to have coffee with a guy. Have you fainted yet? I will tell you all about it at Group tonight. See you later."

Kristy, Diana, and Jessica arrive early. They sit on a row of black chairs in the waiting room. Their voices and giggles fill the room with promise tonight. They are rowdier than usual. At eight o'clock, they march into my office and sit in their usual seats.

Wendy bounces into the room. Tonight she reminds me of A. A. Milne's Tigger: bouncy, friendly, and wide-eyed. She plunks down her Diet Coke on the table next to her favorite corner on the couch and says, "I want to go first."

Everyone nods, nonverbally and enthusiastically saying, "Yeah, go for it."

"Okay, guys, you won't believe this," Wendy begins, "but I went on a date."

My palms begin to sweat. I feel like an anxious mother waiting to hear about Wendy's first date since she was raped twelve years ago.

"I told you guys last week about this person I met on a dating site. We both work with children. I thought it's good that we have something in common. I felt brave, so I agreed to meet him for coffee."

I notice that the eyes of the other women in Group are locked on Wendy. We all know how much is at stake. The sexual assault eroded Wendy's confidence. Men have frightened her ever since. The idea of dating freaked her out. She did not believe she could accurately judge who was dangerous and who was not.

Wendy continues, "I decide that, to be safe, I would meet him in a public place, a place that I know well."

I am relieved that she is thinking about how to protect herself.

"I picked Barnes & Noble to meet him. I figured there would be a lot of people at night sitting around drinking coffee. Before I left to meet him, I called two friends. I wanted them to know where I would be and what time I was meeting this guy. I told them I would call them after the date. I figured if they didn't hear from me, they would come looking for me."

This is good, I think. She is reaching out to others who care about her to create a safety net, something she never had when she was young. She is fixing something devastatingly broken from her past and trying to create a very different outcome.

"So the guy shows up at 8:15. I notice he is fifteen minutes late. I am practicing noticing things about people and about how they act with me. I didn't want to make too big a deal of what I noticed, but I didn't want to ignore it either." Wendy looks at me. "Pretty good, huh?"

I smile. Wendy is practicing her new ability to sense, to pay attention to the signs that denote trustworthiness or danger.

Awareness is replacing the blindness to betrayals that crippled her judgment in the past.

"He was okay looking, sort of clean-cut with glasses and well shaven, not creepy looking, no tattoos or anything, but then again, the guy who raped me wasn't dressed in wolf's clothing. He was also kind of nice looking."

Jessica says, "Your eyes are really open. I am so glad you are thinking about how to be safe."

"We both ordered a cappuccino," Wendy says. "He smiled at me and said he liked redheads. I wanted to cover my hair with my wool scarf but I refrained. We talked, the getting-to-know-each-other kind of stuff. We shared our frustrations with our supervisors at work and all the frustrations of organizations that lack adequate resources to really help children. Things were pretty comfortable for the first fifteen minutes, and then a voice came over the loudspeaker and said, 'Barnes & Noble is closing in ten minutes.' I got nervous. My plan was that we would just hang out at the bookstore.

"We put on our jackets and went outside. And then the dude said, 'Hey, it's kind of chilly. Why don't we go to your place to warm up?' And I said, 'No, we are not going to my place.' And I added, in case he didn't get it, 'That is not going to happen.'"

Kristy and Jessica give Wendy a thumbs-up. Wendy grins.

"Then he reached for my hand. I thought to myself, *I don't know him well enough to hold hands*, so I moved my hand away and put it in my pocket. He asked me where I parked my car. I lied and pointed three blocks west. He said he was cold and repeated, 'Let's go to your place and warm up.'"

I am rooting for Wendy, hoping all the work we have done has armed her with the skills she needed at this moment.

Wendy smiles. "Then I told the dude, 'I think if you're so cold, you better go home and warm up.'"

"You did great," I say clumsily.

She continues, ignoring my enthusiasm. "We got to the train, and he tried to kiss me. I turned my head and said good-bye. I slowly walked back to my car, which was actually right in front of Barnes & Noble. I watched the train pull out of the station, and then I called my friend on my cell phone. She asked, 'Are you still on your date?'

"'Nope,' I said.

"'That was a really short date,' she said, so I told her what happened. We agreed this guy was definitely a creep. But the funny thing is that when I got home, I was so excited about the date. You would have thought someone proposed to me. I felt so proud, so strong and confident, like I can do this. I can really trust myself."

I feel proud, too. My apprehension transforms into an impulse to jump up and down and yell, "Yes!" A large smile shamelessly appears on my face. All of us in the room are smiling.

Wendy has begun to understand that trust needs to be earned. It is not to be granted, as her mother insisted, because someone is given the status of family. Her brother sexually abused her, her sister bullied and physically abused her, and her mother neglected her children. Wendy has broken the spell of silence and secrets that her family required. She is now free to develop a new story about trust and to find the tools and friendships that would help her stay out of harm's way.

Kristy goes next. She places her knitting needles and the beginning of a soft, white baby blanket she is making for a friend in her lap. "You are so brave," she tells Wendy. Kristy is now able to express kindness and compassion to her fellow travelers in Group. Connections with others no longer frighten her.

She smiles and says, "I had a real success this week, too."

"Do tell," Wendy says.

"I took my two boys to a restaurant. They ordered chicken nuggets, and I ordered a rare hamburger. When lunch was set on the table, I cut into my hamburger and it was well done. This may sound really silly, but I did the most amazing thing. I asked the waiter to take it back. I told him that I wanted my hamburger rare, as I had ordered. He did it! He took it back and brought me a yummy rare hamburger! I was thrilled. I felt brave and so grown up."

"Kristy," I say, "what was so exciting about asking the waiter to bring you what you had ordered?"

"In the past, I would have never complained or felt entitled to say that I was displeased. I never would have asked for what I really wanted. I am so used to not being heard. My protests when my father was an asshole, when he hurt me, were constantly ignored and ridiculed. He just kept doing what he wanted, and my mother stood passively by and said nothing."

The triumph isn't the rare hamburger. It is Kristy's new sense of self, the shift from her trauma-informed worldview of ignored protests and silencing to her newfound voice and belief that she can say what she wants and what she thinks. She can protest when something is wrong.

When you're loved, you are not silenced. Protests are heard and respected.

Kristy continues to explain this change in her life. "Sometimes I have to pinch myself. I can't believe this is truly my life. I can buy a quart of raspberries whenever I want, even in the off-season. All three of my kids take for granted that they are safe and loved. I love being with them and, surprisingly, they want to be with me. I love my messy house: the art projects, hockey sticks, and running shoes all over my home. I never imagined life could be this good."

"That is great, Kristy," Diana says. "When you talk about your kids, I secretly wish I had a mom like you."

Kristy grins. There is nothing that she wants more than to be a good, protective, capable mother.

I love watching Kristy treasure the things in life that matter. Once she found the task of parenting daunting; now it is her greatest pleasure. I am in awe, even at moments envious, of her capacities as a mother. She is more than a good-enough mom. Each of her children is like a piece of art to her. She sees their flaws only as further evidence of their beauty and uniqueness. She is also a woman who is getting to know her own desires and wishes.

"I wonder if I will ever feel as hopeful as Kristy," Diana says. "Mostly, I feel angry at everyone."

"Like who?" I ask.

"I am angry at my upstairs neighbors, who never groom their long-haired Chihuahua. They let their damn dog roam in the yard without checking to see if the gate is closed. I am angry at the neighbors with the six-year-old girl who does nothing but rock back and forth on the back porch chair after school. She's sad and lonely. Any fool can see she is starving for attention. When I get home from work, I pick up Queeny at her doggy day care. We're both tired. The girl climbs over my fence. She asks if she can play with Queeny and me. I have to tell her, 'This is not a good time. You can come back after dinner and visit.' Inside, I am raging. I want to say, 'Where the hell are your parents? Why is no one watching you?'"

Diana smells neglect—a dog whose owner doesn't adequately attend to its safety; a small girl who rocks to soothe herself. An infected wound from Diana's past is festering. Her rage spills onto her neighbors. The rage that was unspoken and unacknowledged in her past is appearing in code all around her.

"Diana, you are describing crippling neglect, people who are not attending to their pet or their child," I say. "What do you make of that?"

She shifts effortlessly from the present to the past, as if she were waiting for a cue. "Where was she? How could my mother have turned away?" she exclaims. She pauses and returns to the present. "Last week, my mother came to visit me from Virginia. It had been a long time since she had come to Chicago to visit me. I fixed my bedroom for her, and I slept on the couch."

Diana took her mother to a neighborhood food festival to

listen to music, eat some local food, and enjoy the summer air. After Diana drank a couple of beers and her mother had a margarita, they settled into some folding chairs in the shade.

"I summoned up my courage to ask my mother the question I have always wanted to ask her but didn't dare. I took a deep breath—the two beers helped—and asked, 'How is it you did not know what was going on in our house when I was a kid?' We both knew I was referring to the years when my stepfather sexually abused me. My mother looked away for a moment and then she said, 'That is a regret I will carry to my grave. I worked hard to make money to support you and your brother. Jack stayed home to take care of you. I was so worried about having a roof over our heads. I did not want you and your brother to end up living in the street.'

"Then I said, 'You mean keeping *his* roof over our heads.'"

Diana was glad that her sunglasses hid her tears from her mother's sight. Today in Group, she cringes, recalling the control her stepfather, Jack, had over her. He enrolled her in a Catholic school across town; he drove her to and from school every day. He did not let her out of his sight.

"Neither of us dared to say more," Diana continues, "but at least I broke our deep-seated silence."

What happens next startles and pleases me. Diana expresses something she has never revealed before.

"I really wanted her," she says. "I really wanted my mother to take care of me, and I still do." She lets us see her tears.

Diana looks up at Kristy, her favorite Group member, and adds, "I want more connection with people, and I hate wanting it. I think I want to have sex with someone who loves me. Not just sex for recreation or sport. This is so unsettling."

Kristy smiles and reaches for Diana; Diana extends her hand to Kristy. For the next several minutes, they sit quietly, holding each other's hands. All of us are silent; words are inadequate and unnecessary to honor what we have been allowed to witness tonight.

Diana has never before dared to feel the pain of her mother's failure to love and protect her, let alone allowed others to witness her loss. Something so crucial, so profound, has shifted in Diana. The arm she extended toward Kristy has penetrated the barrier that sustains her treasured but troublesome isolation, her I-depend-on-myself-thank-you-very-much persona is beginning to melt. In a moment of truth and vulnerability, Diana has chosen connection. She has moved toward, not away from, the radiating warmth and caring of a friend.

After a few sacred moments, I ask if there is anything else anyone wants to say or talk about. Jessica says she does.

"Okay, we only have about five minutes left," I say to make sure that we can respond adequately to what she wants to say.

"Oh, that's fine. Everyone tonight talked about these big leaps. I wanted to share something, too. Harry has been real sweet lately. He has been going to therapy for a while. He can really listen to me about my abuse without even trying to fix it. So I have been feeling more comfortable with him. I am thinking about inviting him back into my, well I guess what was *our,* bedroom."

"That would be nice," I say. "You have both come far."

Jessica says she is still afraid that being close will remind her of the scary men from her past.

"I hope that you will be able to differentiate between the men that hurt you in the past and what is happening in your life now. I hope that you can enjoy the comfort of having the husband you have come to trust next to you in bed. I hope that you can remember and honor the horrors of the past, but those memories can live in the past rather than intrude in the tender moments between you and your husband."

"I want that, too," Jessica says.

The hands of the clock reach 10:00 P.M. The footprints of repair are all over the room: Wendy's triumphant date, Kristy's newfound assertiveness at a restaurant, Diana's conversation with her mother, Jessica's estranged husband welcomed back into the bedroom.

At the end of Group tonight, Jessica says, "I have this new thought about change." She pauses. "I think sometimes the small things are really the big things."

Chapter 33: TRANSITIONS

My marriage was over. I was now a single parent. It was my job alone to pay the bills and to recover from the fallout from my divorce.

There were some bright sides. Freedom from Robert's outbursts and unpredictability was a relief. But just to keep life interesting, my best friend's eighteen-year-old daughter, Madeleine, moved into our basement as a kind of halfway house to independence.

Rebuilding a good life for Emily, now nine years old, and Matthew, now twelve, was my first task. I was fortunate to have good friends who provided an ear when needed and watched the kids at a moment's notice if I had an emergency at work.

The children needed me, and I needed them. I had to redefine our family with a diminished bank account. I worked hard to make more money to afford the house my children called home.

Tuesday nights were our special family nights. The children were responsible for making dinner. I supplied the money for groceries, but the rest was up to them. There were no culinary expectations; the only requirement was that they do it together.

The first few Tuesdays had a macaroni-and-cheese theme. One dinner consisted of three different varieties of mac and cheese, with a side of grilled cheese sandwiches and potato chips. The kids happily cooked dinner, set the table, and did the dishes. I took pleasure in their collective efforts.

Soon we added another rule to Tuesday night dinners: guests were welcome as long as they participated in some aspect of the meal. My children began to bring their friends. Soon stray kids from the neighborhood were chopping vegetables for a salad, mopping the floor, or running to the grocery store for a forgotten ingredient. Matthew's best friend Jake was a regular, sometimes dragging along his six-year-old brother, Joey, who was responsible for putting napkins on a table he could barely reach on his tiptoes.

Ricardo, a kid with a glass eye who struggled to stay in high school, was an occasional guest. On his first visit, Ricardo plopped himself down, ready for a free meal. Afterward, as he got ready to leave, one of the regulars called out, "Hey, Ricardo. You're on dishes tonight." Ricardo was stunned. He whispered, "I've never done dishes." I assured him I would teach him everything he needed to know. He smiled and rolled up his sleeves.

Our home was bustling with activity. But in spite of school, extracurricular activities, work emergencies, and even Matthew's football practice, nothing ever interfered with our Tuesday night dinners. We were more clan than conventional family, but on Tuesday nights there was no doubt where we belonged and what mattered.

Three years after Robert left, I reluctantly began to date again. Dan, a friend from college, and I began to see each other. He knew that the wounds from my divorce were still festering. My favorite times with Dan were when we walked along the lakefront holding hands. I felt ready for the romantic expectations of a fifteen-year-old girl.

Dan always let me set the pace; he never pushed. I felt safe.

After several months, we ventured into gentle sexual foreplay. The surges of pleasure and sexual arousal I experienced were new, exciting, and healing. One night, when the kids were with their father, Dan asked me if I wanted to spend the night at his apartment in downtown Chicago. I had come to love being physically close to him; his body was soft, inviting, and responsive to my touch.

In a moment devoid of maturity, I decided that after dinner we could drive to his apartment and, if a parking space happened to be free in front of his building, it would be a sign that I should spend the night. If there was no parking space, clearly I should go home.

The chances of there being a parking space on a Saturday night in Dan's yuppie Chicago neighborhood were slight—but just as we approached his apartment building, a silver Toyota pulled out of a space right in front. Dan parked.

Excited and scared, I walked up the stairs to his bachelor sanctuary.

He opened the door. A coffee cup with yesterday's coffee sat on the breakfast table, and a collection of newspapers—*The Wall Street Journal*, *The New York Times*, and the *Chicago Tribune*—covered every inch of his living room floor. Dan offered me coffee, but finding a clean cup was impossible. He put on some music; we talked, laughed, and kissed. The sound of honking cars and screeching "L" trains rose from the street through the unwashed windows.

Later that evening, as I lay naked on his queen-sized bed, I began to shake and cry, obliterating the romantic mood. "I am sorry," I say crying softly, "but I don't think I can do this."

Dan stroked my head gently. "That's fine. I just like being here next to you."

I believed him. He held me in his arms, and I fell asleep listening to the late-night noises of the city streets.

I continued seeing Dan. The next time, I was less afraid,

and my sexual desire continued to awaken. My body stopped shaking. Sex with Dan was comforting, passionate, and deeply healing. He was exciting, kind, smart, and unreliable. But he also treasured his freedom above the comfort and predictable company of a loved one.

With Dan, I discovered the silly glow common in young women who know the flush from good sex. But I was not a young woman; I was forty years old and divorced, with children who waited up for me.

———

Twice a week, Robert picked up the kids for dinner and then brought them back to the house to sleep. Robert slept on his friends' couches, or with a girlfriend. My house was the kids' home.

When Matthew was ready to start high school, Robert rented an apartment several blocks from my house. One Monday evening, he called to inform me that he wanted Matthew to live with him. He said he would pick up Matthew and his belongings that Friday.

I hung up the phone and doubled over, sobbing. I slid down to the floor, bracing myself on the handle of our refrigerator, which was adorned with Emily and Matthew's artwork. A piercing ache shot through me; I thought I might pass out.

I had bought Matthew his first pair of blue jeans. I'd had the mother-son talk with him when I discovered him with his first *Playboy* magazine. I'd taken him to the emergency room when he broke his arm playing on the playground. I'd comforted him when a bully taunted him on the school bus. I was the one who had waited for him at the bus stop every day after school with his favorite snack. But in the arena of custody, those things don't count. The natural parent's rights always trump the stepparent's. Legally, I had no say about Matthew leaving my home or where he would live.

Four days later, Robert pulled up to our house in his blue

Honda with the dented passenger door. I heard the annoying honking of his horn. Matthew stood in the doorway with his boom box under his arm. He looked stunned. Without looking at me, he opened the front door, walked down the stone path, and slid into the passenger seat of his father's car.

A tidal wave of grief washed over me. I fell asleep in my clothes after dinner. I awoke fourteen hours later, my patchwork quilt soaked in tears and sweat.

Matthew continued to come for Tuesday dinners when he could. I took solace days when I found the previous night's leftovers had been eaten, recognizing the evidence of Matthew's visit in the refrigerator.

The depth of my pain and the extent of my resilience stunned me. My grief arose at unwelcomed ordinary moments: when I was checking out with fewer groceries, when I sat next to only one child at the movies on a Sunday, or when a client told me about losing someone precious. Sadness so primitive, so pure, and so surprising could erupt in those moments and knock me off balance.

My stamina, my professional success, the care of friends, and the warmth of my home were constant sources of soothing. I asked Emily if she ever wished her dad and I would get back together. She did not hesitate. "No, this is better, Mom. I get to see my dad and Matthew and live here with you."

Chapter 34: KRISTY'S WINGS

Many small things have changed over the years. The water cooler in the waiting room now has cold and hot water. The arms of the nubby white couch in the waiting room are grey from the sweat from clients who've sat there happily, nervously, or resentfully anticipating their therapy sessions. The walls are freshly painted. Grey and white tweed chairs have replaced the tattered tan chairs in the Group room.

Large things have changed, too. Kristy's hair is now styled in layers, so when she runs her fingers through it, she has a wind-blown look. Her clothes are less monotone. Her silver sweater looks nice with her charcoal pants. Her toenails are painted, and she sometimes wears jewelry—nothing fancy, just silver earrings that dangle a bit. She sits taller and looks more vibrant. She often hugs me at the end of our therapy sessions, which was once unthinkable.

Kristy is still unencumbered by traditional expectations, which frightens and pleases her. She joined a women's ice hockey team, where she discovered the energy and catharsis that come from knocking her opponents forcefully into the side of the rink.

She enjoys the camaraderie with her teammates and occasionally deceives her husband about when her games end so she can join them for a quick beer afterward.

She has created a studio in her basement where she turns glass beads into works of art. She joined a church, because she wanted to be part of a community of people who care about helping others. She was mortified when the pastor invited her to volunteer for a ceremonial task at the Sunday services, but volunteered to make a stained glass window for the church's rickety front door.

Kristy has come so far from her childhood of neglect. She has found her interests and her voice, and discovered how capable she is. She giggles with joy as she tells me how she sent the appliance repairman away because she wanted to try fixing the washing machine herself.

Where she really shines, through, is where it matters most: parenting her three children, two are now teenagers. "Raising yourself—or rather, becoming a person—at the same time you raise your kids is not always easy," Kristy says. "But I needed to, for me and for my children." She wants them to have a mom who likes herself, who knows how to navigate the social world, who understands what matters and what doesn't. "Maybe I haven't given them a model of a great marriage, but I do know that my children never doubt they are loved and that there is someone watching out for them," she says.

Kristy knows the kind of parent she will not be: a clueless one. She wants to be a good-enough mom, and in my opinion, she has far surpassed that expectation.

Kristy supports her children's strengths and attends to their vulnerabilities and needs. Max, with his perfect SAT scores and straight A's, needed an extra shot of humility, Kristy thought. So she volunteered him to tutor younger children in reading. She was not disappointed when Yale University rejected his college application. "Everything came so easily to Max," she explains.

"I want him to know that everything will not just be handed to him. I want him to be able to deal with disappointments, too."

Kristy used to worry about her daughter, Josie, the most. Josie needed coaching on social strategies. So Kristy encouraged her to notice who was nice and who knew how to be a good friend, rather than focus on the popular girls. When Josie got depressed in high school, she sought out the school counselor for help and told Kristy afterward. "I was so proud of her for being brave, for asking for help, that I sent her flowers," Kristy says.

Sweet-tempered Willy, her youngest, needed extra love. He could get lost in the shiny glow of his siblings. Kristy made sure he was also recognized for his accomplishments. She went to his swim meets—which, honestly, she hated—because she wanted Willy to know that he mattered and she would be there, cheering for him.

———

When Kristy first became my client, I talked to her about joining Group in addition to her individual therapy. I told her that Group was a good place to learn how to turn to others for support rather than isolate herself when she was distressed. "I don't get what you're talking about; isn't that all backwards, kind of absurd?" she asked me at the time. "It's like you're telling someone who is thirsty that they may want to try Chinese water torture."

That has changed, too.

Others have come and gone from Group, but Kristy has been a steady presence. The women in Group have witnessed each other's wounds and triumphs. This random assortment of souls, once strangers, has become a mutual lifeline.

"I first came to Group when my daughter was seven years old; now she is sixteen," Kristy reflects. "I like my life. I like everything about it. I had no good friendships when I came to Group, and now I have three really good friendships. I feel like a rich person."

Tonight at Group, Kristy starts.

"I want to tell all of you what happened this week," she says. "It is not earth-shaking, but I learned everything I did from being here with you guys. My friend Sally came home from chemo to her three children; my friends and I signed up to take shifts cooking and bringing her meals. On the way to take my daughter to her softball practice, I realized this was my night to bring dinner. I called a friend sobbing. She was alarmed and asked me what was wrong. I blurted, 'I forgot to get dinner for Sally and to bring it to her.' I told her I was so mortified and upset. But my friend was relieved. She thought there was something terribly wrong, like something of shattering proportions wrong. She said to me, 'Don't worry. I can run over and take her something tonight.' She was so reassuring."

Kristy looks up at the ceiling. "I never would have reached out before. I never would have allowed anyone to see me that upset. I would have told myself over and over that I was a total fuck-up. Then I would have crawled under the covers and hoped I didn't wake up. Now, I rally."

Kristy repaid the favor the following day by bringing her friend a thank-you note and a basket of sandwiches. "I messed up, but my friend was there and she didn't hate me, and I could fix what went wrong," Kristy says. She now embraces and practices a new formula, one based not on perfection but on the possibility of repair, with accountability, responsibility, and amends. Kristy now walks on a new path, one that fosters enduring connections with others.

"I love you guys so much," she says. "The bad news is . . ." She takes a deep breath. "In three weeks I am going to leave and try my wings."

There is a hush in the room until Jessica recovers and asks, "How do you know you are really ready to leave Group?"

"When I began in Group, I didn't have any mutual friendships, like where I cared about someone and they also cared about me," Kristy replies. "I didn't know about boundaries. My relationships were exhausting and frightening. Now I can say 'no.' I used to think you just try to figure out the rules and then do what is expected. Now I listen to myself, and there is something inside to tell me which way to turn. I learned that here." She blinks back tears. "When my kids ask me stuff, I feel like a real grown-up. Sometimes I hear Laurie's voice. This week, when my daughter didn't want to do something that I thought was important, it was like Laurie was hiding under my sink. The voice under the sink said, *Remember the grey*. I told my daughter she had to go to an event she did not want to go to, but I would help her figure out how it could be less awful for her. Josie said she was uncomfortable around the girl whose mother was going to drive them to the event. 'You could go in another car or I could drive you, if that would help,' I told her. We worked it out. That's a miracle. I feel confident as a mom, like I can make good decisions, teach my kids what's right, and respect them, too. I am not sure why I am crying—maybe 'cause I feel proud. That is such an unfamiliar feeling for me."

Jessica responds, "I wish I was as giving with people as you are. I am still in too much pain from the past. Your words of encouragement always help me. I will miss you, but I am glad you are who you are and that you are doing so well. I find it hopeful."

Carrie adds, "I will miss you, too." She admits she is angry about Kristy leaving. "There is part of me that wants to say, 'If you're leaving in three weeks, why don't you just leave now?'"

Kristy smiles. She knows those feelings.

"I don't know about the grey yet," Wendy says. "Maybe some shades of black and white, but not grey. I am just starting to learn how and whom to trust. I can see how much you have changed even in the short time I've been here. I'm glad for you and sad for us. I'm not sure I have ever felt love or that I even know how to recognize it if it shows up."

Kristy replies, "I never used to be able to feel loved either, but now I can." She looks at Wendy with confidence. "You'll get there."

I look at the wet faces around the room and dry my own eyes. I feel as though I could weep with joy, loss, and pride. I love the life Kristy now enjoys. Her spirit is strong because she has healed and learned about relationships that are sustaining, not abusive or devoid of care. Her relationships are life giving and many other people also are better off because of it. What a privilege it is to have witnessed Kristy's determination to become a woman worthy of her children's love and admiration.

———

Kristy now comes to see me twice a month to check in about her kids and talk to me about her marriage. Kristy married Rich "before"—before children, before she awoke, before she found herself. He is a good father and provider, but some things trouble her about him and about their marriage. For the last decade, she has solely focused on being a good mother to her children and finding herself. But now the kids are older and need her less. Her marriage and its flaws have floated to the forefront. Some things, like his smoking, she has learned to live with, but other things disturb her. She has begun to worry about her marriage, about being with Rich when the kids are gone.

"I hate when he's unhappy and complains," she says. "I want to say, 'Get over it. We have a good life.' Or I want to tell him, 'If you are so dissatisfied, you should fucking do something about it.'"

I wonder aloud why Kristy is edgy and less compassionate when she talks about her husband. Kristy wonders, too.

"What is it about his attitude that you find so distasteful?" I ask.

"I hate his stuckness, his powerlessness," she replies, beginning to see a connection. "My father was such a loser. He was always unhappy and complaining and never did anything about it. He was such a victim, and he sucked sympathy from everyone. I thought he was pathetic. I remember when he took me to a father-daughter dance, and I realized he just wasn't like the other dads. He was broken."

"And Rich, do you see him as broken?"

"No, he does a lot for the family. He is involved with his kids. He goes running with Max and shows up at Willy's swim meets." She pauses. "Okay, so I should be nicer to him."

"It's not just about nicer," I reply. "If you want to work on your marriage, you may want to learn to talk to Rich in a way that might invite him to be more receptive, more open to hearing you."

"Like, how do you do that?" she asks.

"Well, you might acknowledge more vulnerability. You could say something like, 'I really want us to have a good marriage. I want a marriage that works for both of us. There are some things that I wish were different, and I imagine there are things that you wish were different. I want us to be able to talk about things with each other.'"

"Oh," Kristy says, smiling impishly. "You think that might work better than, 'Why don't you pull up your fucking pants, grow up, and have some self-respect?'" She smiles. "I know it's not all him and I have to work at this, too." She looks softer, sadder. "I really do care about him."

"I know you do."

Chapter 35: A DIFFERENT KIND OF LOVE

Michael was nervous. A spread of hummus, falafel, and pita bread sat untouched on the table. This was our first date. We belonged to the same club: betrayed, recently divorced, with children. Conversation was easy—politics, being a single parent—but there were definitely no sparks.

I was not ready for a serious relationship, and even if I were, Michael would not be a suitable candidate. He had two children, ages four and six. I was not interested in falling in love with someone else's children again.

He was also short, nervous, and younger than I was. And to further confirm my less than favorable impressions, he rode his bicycle to lunch and didn't realize his helmet was still on his head for the first twenty minutes of our date.

He definitely was not cool.

———

Michael and I continued to meet for an occasional lunch or dinner. We rode our bikes on the lakefront path from time to time. In the aftermath of divorce, companionship is soothing.

Michael always returned my phone calls promptly. He showed up on time and he was interested in my life and in me. We exchanged stories about our children. My daughter was becoming a teenager; his were barely in grade school. As a single mom with a private therapy practice, my income was unpredictable. I worried about having enough money to pay my bills. Michael, a professor with a steady paycheck, had no concerns about money. He said he was wealthy. This surprised me. Professors do not have huge salaries. I wondered if he had a special trust fund or an inheritance from a deceased relative. Neither was true. He was wealthy, he explained, because he had everything he needed or wanted.

I felt blessed and tortured in my life; Michael felt only blessed, though he did not use that term. We both loved our work. My clients shared their wishes, dreams, and injuries with me. I was enamored of both the craft of psychotherapy and art of training and teaching therapists. Michael was accomplished in his field, but he was uninterested in status or the acclaim of others. As an engineer, he focused on the joy of solving puzzles. What he liked best about his job was the flexibility it provided, allowing him to take his children to their doctor appointments in the middle of the day or volunteer at their science fairs. He was on the board of his youngest daughter's daycare center, where he helped raise money so children in need could attend. In his spare time, he worked for a progressive local candidate and co-sponsored a proposal for the neighborhood public schools to ensure that minorities had access to the best schools.

He was not conflicted when a professional ambition collided with the needs of his children; the children came first.

Meanwhile, I continued occasional late-night rendezvous with Dan. We enjoyed each other's company. He was charming, smart, and averse to responsibility—familiar patterns in the men I had loved. By contrast, Michael lacked the showy charisma that typically led me into intense infatuation followed by betrayal, the pattern that was hardwired in my brain from my childhood.

One weeknight after work, I met Michael for dinner at a Chinese restaurant. This time, he remembered to remove his bicycle helmet. As we shared some chicken chow mein, Michael casually mentioned that he had begun dating someone. Michael and I were not really dating, just getting together as friends, but I felt a tinge of jealousy.

Surprisingly, a voice from above—or below, or inside of me—whispered in my ear. Barely audible at first, I think the voice murmured something like, *This is a good man. He is trustworthy; he lives the values you admire. Why not choose someone like this to love?* It seemed preposterous, counter to my deeply embedded instincts. Could I appreciate, or even tolerate, someone who was loyal, attentive, and reliable?

In a moment of panic, I called my good friend in Boston who was also recently divorced and a father with a teenage daughter.

"Jeff, I met this man. This is terrible, but I think I like him."

"Hey, Laurie, slow down," Jeff said in a soft, reassuring tone. "What is so terrible about this man?"

"He has two daughters." Then I raised my voice for emphasis. "They are four and seven years old. He is shorter, younger, and nicer than me. This is not what I had in mind. This is so complicated!"

"Laurie," my dear, wise friend replied, "at our age, you get complicated or dead."

I continued to feel ambivalent about my relationship with Michael. Michael was sure that love and marriage were the golden charm. I thought it was equally possible that the golden charm was really a grenade that could explode in your hand without notice. Michael was eager to love and be loved, and I was reluctant. He and I had learned different lessons about love from our families. His parents' favorite activity was coming over and watching the children play. They did not require a meal or the making of an occasion of any significance. His mother was indifferent to his messy house. They were both content—actually, pleased—as long as they could be in the presence of their family and the sticky hands and dirty faces of their grandchildren. The children would finger paint on their grandfather's bald head. Michael's father, a distinguished physicist by day, would sit on the floor with blue paint dripping down to his ears, a contented smile on his face. Michael's parents believed that family was the most sacred of the sacred. They intrigued me. Their devotion to their children and grandchildren appeared effortless.

Besides loving their grandchildren, Michael's mother and father could be caught looking adoringly at each other from across the dinner table. During the summers, they put a canoe on the roof of their car and drove to upstate New York to camp on an island for a month. In matching sleeping bags under the stars, they were more than content. They referred to their summer camping trip as their annual honeymoon. The children and grandchildren sometimes came to the island to share their paradise. They entertained themselves by canoeing, hiking, and—his mother's favorite—hunting for edible mushrooms.

I had never been on a family vacation. I have no memories of being read to at night or playing games with my parents. I had a dog I loved, and dance and piano lessons after school, but those were things separate from my parents.

While some people are crippled by trauma, others make meaning from their suffering and construct lives that are testimonies to something better. At the age of seven, Michael's mother escaped from Nazi Germany with her mother. They traveled by boat with few possessions. Michael's grandmother worked long hours to support her daughter in America. In Chicago, they found a small apartment in the Home Club, an intentional community for single mothers. Michael's grandmother worked long hours and joined the International Ladies' Garment Workers' Union. Michael's mother grew up poor, but she was never impoverished in love.

Michael believed a healthy woman with good self-esteem

was sexy; he liked women with a sense of self and ambitions of their own. What he liked best was sharing every day with someone. When it came to those he loved, he was generous with his time and investment.

I knew enough about love by now to listen to this new voice inside of me. I was willing to consider discarding the script about love that I'd learned as a child and walk into unfamiliar territory.

Michael and I continued to date. Emily, now twelve, immediately disliked him. I was her touchstone. She did not want anyone interfering with what we had together or disturbing the place she called home.

Michael's house resembled a nursery school. Four small blue plastic chairs and a matching miniature table furnished the living room; an easel graced the hallway; the children's toys and books covered every visible surface. The kitchen table was adorned with red and yellow blobs of Play-Doh, which the children insisted were houses. They did not own a television. There was no couch a person over four feet tall could sit on. The only pictures on the walls were colorful drawings, to use the term loosely, created by the children. One of the children's favorite games was what they called "night cleaners." They would set an alarm for midnight and get up to clean their rooms. This was a very strange family.

Michael's daughters took great comfort in playing with each other. Their imaginations had no bounds; they played for hours while the rest of the world vanished. Some days, they were space aliens discovering distant planets or detectives solving a crime. They created a language of their own and made up lyrics to songs. One day, while I was visiting Michael, the girls created colorful posters and, with the help of their father, glued them to sticks. One read "Save the Dolphins." They happily walked back and forth in front of the house in a two-person protest march. They did not mind when I was around; mostly, they didn't notice.

Emily was five-foot-nine. Matthew, a frequent visitor, was now the captain of the football team, with the physique to match. Michael's daughters were the shortest kids in their classes. Michael was concerned that my kids would accidently step on his children and squish them.

That was just the start of their differences. While Michael's daughters, Danielle and Ariana, had never watched TV, my kids knew the name of every actor and could recite entire dialogues from their favorite television shows. Michael's daughters were wholesome. My kids were funny, edgy, and mischievous. This was not a match made in heaven.

Fortunately, Emily adored the girls, and they found her intriguing and exotic. Danielle would sneak down to Emily's teenage bedroom in the basement, where the floor was covered with books, CDs, and clothes. On the wall behind her bed was a dark mural with quotes from her favorite Grunge songs. Emily would keep Danielle up late, reading her stories from her favorite Anne Rice novels, The Vampire Chronicles. Emily asked if the girls could live with us and if we could get rid of Michael.

———

That summer, Emily and I went to New York to visit my mother and her husband of ten years, who had been diagnosed with lymphoma that was rapidly spreading though his body. I loved the smell of summer in the city and the energy of New Yorkers rushing around. My mother, Emily, and I took my stepfather to his favorite restaurant for dinner. I held his arm, steadying him as we walked the two blocks. In the middle of the meal, he felt faint and we rushed him to the hospital. Emily insisted on kissing him good night before we left. That evening, he died. I held my mother as she wept, the two of us on her king-size bed in her bright yellow bedroom.

I called Michael in the morning to tell him my stepfather had died. He asked if he should come to New York. I said it wasn't necessary; he had met my stepfather only once before.

I went to the funeral home with my stepfather's son for the surreal task of picking out a casket. The funeral director, who guided us through his collection of caskets, was part charm and part used car salesman. When I returned to my mother's apartment, I sat at the antique desk in the den with a mixture of exhaustion and adrenaline, trying to write my thoughts about my stepfather to read at his funeral the next day.

Two hours before the memorial service, the doorbell rang. When I opened the door, Michael was standing there. "I wanted to be here with you," he said. I stared at him for a long minute then hugged him. My doubts about our relationship dissolved. This time, I realized, I could fall in love with a man who had character and loyalty rather than charm.

Emily and Michael struggled to create a relationship. Slowly, Emily began to depend on Michael; she would call him at work with questions about her computer, and later, when she could drive, she called with questions about her beat-up car that had constant mechanical difficulties. She began to notice that he was someone she could rely on. One day, Emily called Michael from a police station, crying. While driving to her summer job as a camp counselor, she had run a stop sign. The police had pulled her over and found a trace of marijuana in the ashtray. She had been arrested and handcuffed.

Michael left work immediately, drove forty-five minutes, and bailed her out of jail. He did not lecture her or shame her in any way. He comforted her and drove her to camp, and together they figured out a plan to get her car back.

Michael and I got married the next summer. Emily, Matthew, and Michael's daughters all gave us their blessings.

Chapter 36: JESSICA GOES TO CAMBODIA

Jessica has become interested in the issues of human trafficking—not surprising, given her history. I am pleased she is thinking and learning about global issues, the context, *her* context.

Jessica and I have worked hard for many years and accomplished a lot. Together we have forged a safe, enduring relationship. As a child, Jessica had no adults she could rely on; her sister was the only one who ever comforted her. "This thing called attachment, I don't think I ever felt it before I met you," she says.

A safe attachment is the crucible of human development. But even some experienced therapists keep their eyes glued to the traumatic experience and its impact and pay too little attention to the equally devastating impact of the early attachment trauma. Most of my clients, including Jessica, experience what we call disorganized attachment. Their caretakers, who were supposed to be sources of comfort and safety were not. Instead their caretakers frightened them. A new experience of attachment is necessary for them to develop the capacities necessary to thrive. "We are a team," I tell Jessica. She beams. More is possible when there is a secure, dependable other.

Jessica has a gentle nature, but her ability to recognize sensations and feelings was lacking. She could not use her feelings to guide her. Now she feels sadness and the more complex feelings of grief. She can rage at her childhood abusers. She is feistier, less compliant. Even more important, she now is able to reflect on her experiences, to think about her thoughts. This is essential for her to understand her past and how it impacts her in the present. It is necessary for her to know that the horrors of past are over and she is now safe. This ability is more intuitive for those who were lucky enough to have safe and secure attachments when they were children. For others, this ability must be fostered.

With the comfort of a trusted other, Jessica has been able to face her childhood; she now has a narrative about her ghastly past. Her relationship with her husband has evolved into a caring, trusting one after a traumatic beginning. She has come far.

But I want more for her. I wanted her to have a bigger life—one with meaning and with more opportunities for using the capacities she has developed. The idea of work, having a job, remains daunting and out of reach.

There is a reason the idea of work is hard for Jessica. When her father took her to the house where men paid for the crime of sexually exploiting young girls, he would say, "It's time to go to work." The very idea of work can throw Jessica into a cascade of nightmares and traumatic memories. But the lack of purpose in her life frustrates her and contributes to her isolation and depression.

Today when Jessica arrives, I notice she is wearing a sweater with a rainbow of jewel colors, very unlike her usual, more muted wardrobe. Her affect is also less muted. Her speech is faster, her eyes brighter than usual.

Earlier this week, she tells me, she attended a conference at DePaul University. "I found this organization that has a vision I believe in," she says. "They want to create a world where women and girls are safe from trafficking and sexual exploitation. After one of the sessions I went to, I met the coordinator of the organization that works with these girls. I told her my story. I said I want to do something to help the girls and help end human trafficking. She said they have a program where volunteers come for three months and work with the girls."

"You look so excited." I am thrilled to see her vitality.

"I am excited. I think I really want to do this."

"Where is this organization?"

"Oh," Jessica says. "I thought I mentioned that. It's in Cambodia."

"Wow, Jessica."

I think about the time, years ago, when Jessica first began to find the words to speak about her past. I remember the extraordinary time when she suggested that we watched the documentary filmed in Phnom Penh, Cambodia, called *Children For Sale*.

"They will interview me again on the phone. I guess they screen people very carefully. I will know in a few weeks."

As the time gets closer, Jessica grows apprehensive. She worries that she will be captured and end up back in a brothel. We work, as we have many times, on the memories that these fears evoke, on her ability to tolerate her feelings, we pace the work so she won't be overwhelmed by her memories or her feelings about the past. I encourage her to notice what she is feeling, to stay present. She is strong enough now to notice and then reflect on her feelings from the past; she knows that these fears, though still powerful, come from something that happened to her long ago. She has learned how to reassure herself that things are different now, that she is safe, and that she has choices she did not have as a child. If she goes to Cambodia, she can take precautions. She can speak with the organization about her safety concerns.

Over time, Jessica calms down, and the wrenching feelings that live in her body subside.

I realize I am invested in Jessica going to Cambodia. I worry I will push her for the wrong reasons, projecting onto her what gives me meaning. Making a difference in the world, in ways big and small, is the core of my spirituality; it is how I understand why I am here and what matters. This does not have to be Jessica's way, but I believe and have witnessed that for those who were once rendered powerless through no fault of their own, agency—the ability to act on behalf of themselves and others—makes a difference. To challenge what is corrupt and seek justice and change enhances their feeling of being a member of the human community. Trauma can rob its victims of meaning and of their instinct of purpose. A survivor mission allows many people to feel whole and worthy. I also hope this might bring Jessica out of the darkness caused by lack of purpose that still occupies too many of her days.

Jessica has another challenge, too: shame.

When children are treated as objects rather than as treasured individuals, they internalize a deep sense of unworthiness and a secret disgust with themselves. "If people who were supposed to protect and love me treated me with such disdain and cruelty, I must be such trash, not fully human," Jessica once told me. This shame is undeserved and unwarranted, but it is the way a child makes meaning of betrayals that are incomprehensible. Cruelty and silence are shame's allies. The victim is blamed, and the perpetrator is freed from culpability.

How can you treasure yourself and others when, instead of taking you to the playground, your father drove you to a house where men sexually abused young girls? Jessica's secret world—the world she was told never to speak about—created a deep sense of dissociation, isolation, and alienation. She needs to find ways to belong, to be seen. She needs to feel valued and whole, and to be of use to others.

I believe in the work we are doing together. I also believe that there are times that more than therapy is needed. This is one of those times. Jessica needs something bigger than the two of us, something with a purpose and a mission connected to the greater human community. She needs to have a role in righting a wrong, to stand up and be heard about larger injustices. This can help diminish the deeply embedded shame she feels as a result of the prolonged and dehumanizing mistreatment she experienced as a child.

———

Jessica receives the news that she has been accepted as an English teacher at one of the shelters in Cambodia. The shelter serves girls who have escaped or been rescued from the clutches of human trafficking and want to build a new life. Jessica is excited but still unsure if this is something she can manage. She asks the coordinator if she can think it over and get back to her in a week.

I know this will be a big leap for Jessica. In the years we have worked together, she has never been away from therapy for more than two weeks at a time. This will be three months. Jessica asks me if we can Skype once a week if she takes the position.

"I would be happy to Skype," I say. "It would be a wonderful way for us to stay in contact."

Jessica smiles faintly. "I want to talk to Harry about this, too. I still have mixed feelings."

"Good. You are taking time to decide; you are listening to yourself. As you come to a decision, use the skills you have and think about what is in the past and what is in the present that scares you."

Jessica nods. She has become an astute student of trauma and healing.

When someone is terrorized over an extended period of time, their central nervous system begins to stay on high alert at all times. Survivors need a new experience of managing fear to replace the automatic fear response from the past. Ironically, survivors often underreact to real threats to their well-being but overreact to imagined threats when they are actually safe.

Jessica reports more nightmares over the next several days. Although they disturb her, she is able to soothe herself and the fear does not linger into the day.

I wonder what she will decide. Secretly, my fingers are crossed, hoping she will choose to go. I want her courage and her passion for justice to win. I believe she is capable, more capable than she has yet discovered.

———

Jessica sits down on the couch. "Hi, Laurie. How are you?"

Jessica always asks how I am before she talks about herself, regardless of the intensity of her distress.

I try to read her face, which I often can—but not today. Then the edges of her mouth turn slightly upward, as if she is about to smile. "I have decided to go to Cambodia. Harry and I talked it over. Harry decided that he would come with me for the first three weeks."

"How wonderful that you and Harry will be able to share part of this adventure," I say. Then I pause for a long moment.

"What are you thinking?" Jessica asks.

"I am thinking that when someone loves you well, they want to support your dreams. I think that is what Harry is doing."

This may be Harry's greatest amends to Jessica. Some years ago, after some coaxing, he acknowledged that having sex with Jessica when she was his patient was wrong. He even wrote it on a piece of paper for her to keep. Now he is staying by her side at a crucial time, a time when his support will enable her to grow and continue to find herself. The coordinator of the program tells Jessica that Harry will not be allowed on the site, but he is not deterred. He wants to do this with her, for her.

I have developed a place in my heart for Harry. I want to say to him, "Bravo." He has learned how to be an ally in Jessica's healing, and he has learned how to be a better man.

It has been several weeks since Jessica and I talked, but she e-mails me frequently with updates. She and Harry had a good time exploring Cambodia together. This week she has begun working at the shelter.

I want Skyping with Jessica to go well. I fuss with my computer. I Skype with my husband to make sure everything is working. I try out headphones to see if that helps with the clarity of the sound. It is early. I have just made my morning cup of coffee. For Jessica, it is nighttime. I want her to feel our connection, my support. I am excited to hear how she is doing and what she has found in this distant land.

"Hi, Laurie. Oops. I can't see you; there's no picture. Oh, it froze. Oh, there you are." Jessica giggles as our faces become visible to each other.

"Can you see me?"

"Yeah, I can."

"This is great."

We are both delighted with this technology, which allows us to be more like neighbors chatting than two people separated by an ocean and 8,600 miles.

Jessica tells me she spent her first week at a shelter with the older girls, the veterans of the program who help with outreach to the girls in the local brothels. The older girls are the backbone of the project; they tell the girls they meet that they can get help and services, and they give them condoms. They speak some English, too.

"These girls are the cream of the crop," Jessica says. "They help recover others from captivity. I have gotten to know them; we have made a good connection. Last night, I was talking to a couple of the girls. They told me that they don't sleep well because of what happened to them during the nighttime in the past and because they know what the girls they talked to during the day are experiencing. I feel close to them. I told them that I know about nighttime when you can't sleep because your past haunts you."

"How wonderful you could be there with them in that way!" I tell her.

Jessica ignores my comment, which is unusual for her, but she has so much on her mind. "I hate Cambodia, but I love the girls I work with and I love the mission of the organization. Cambodia is a hard place to be; it is physically and emotionally hard. The people outside of the shelter relate to me as a visitor. They think that visitors have lots of money. The waiter and the driver tell me their life stories. I realize when they get to the end of their story that the reason that they told me their story is they want me to give them money. They are begging. I don't resent them. I hate their government that keeps them in poverty. I say no about two hundred times a day. Today, someone tried to steal my backpack as they drove by on a motorcycle. There is so much poverty, and the brothels and the clubs where men find young girls for sex are in plain sight."

We pause for technical difficulties.

"Oh, Laurie, your face is hard to see now, I see more of the ceiling than your face. Can you angle your screen differently?"

"How's that?"

"Just a little higher. Oh, that's perfect."

Happily, we are back in each other's view.

Jessica's voice becomes less upbeat. I hear a touch of sadness.

"Yesterday was my last day here with the older girls. I go to the shelter in the countryside tomorrow, where I will spend the next several months teaching English. I am looking forward to going there. I will have more responsibilities, more I can do. But yesterday, saying good-bye was so hard and surprising."

"What was surprising?" I ask, but she continues her story.

"I climbed fifty steps to the classroom, where the girls and the staff were all sitting around a long table waiting for me. Their faces were so sad. I told them I would never forget them and that they were very special. I told them that they have taught me so much and that I will always have a place for them in my heart."

I am struck by Jessica's ability to stand in front of a group and speak so graciously from her heart, transcending the language barrier.

"Then I told them that in America, I don't have any trafficking sisters. 'Why?' they asked. 'Because no one talks about it; it's a big secret in America,' I replied. They all looked at me with this look. Then, in English, almost in one voice, they all said, 'Then we are your sisters.'"

Jessica pauses. "My heart melted," she says. "I felt this feeling of kinship, this feeling I think I have been wanting for such a long time."

I am in awe. Jessica was able to express warmth, respect, and generosity to the girls and the staff, and they reciprocated. During the week she spent with these girls, a connection so precious and meaningful occurred—for her, and for the girls, too.

"I am glad I am here. In Cambodia, the trafficking of girls is so widespread it is talked about, written about in the daily papers. They even have anti-trafficking week; it's recognized in the culture. It's awful, but I find it so freeing that it is not kept secret."

Our time on Skype is coming to an end.

"Tomorrow is a big day," Jessica says. "I have a long bus ride to the shelter, which is in a small village. I will write a note when I get there. Can we Skype the same time next week?"

"Absolutely. I will look forward to it."

"Me too," Jessica says.

The next time, Skype works more easily and Jessica sounds excited and upbeat, eager to tell me what she is doing and discovering.

"How was your trip?" I ask.

"Long," she says. "After the seven-hour bus ride, a tuk tuk driver took me to the shelter. We went over these bumpy, dusty roads. There were a million hogs all over the road, and chickens and oxen and lots of stray dogs. After about twenty minutes, we arrived at the shelter. It is a gated community in the middle of nowhere."

"What an adventure."

"No kidding. There are beetles, spiders, and flies everywhere. There are about fifty girls there—three babies, a three-year-old, and a five-year-old, and then the ages of the other girls range from twelve to twenty. The girls live in three huts, with just a straw mat under them and their feet at the center, like spokes on a wheel."

"Wow, Jessica," I say. "If the shelter were here, it would be closed down."

"Yep, this is a different world." She laughs.

"The babies don't wear diapers," she continues, eager to tell me more. "They just pee or have a bowel movement, and the mothers just wipe it right up. But I have to tell you what is most amazing."

I can't imagine what more she will add that is more amazing.

"What's most amazing is that I feel so comfortable. I feel so normal here. It's weird, really weird, but I fit in, I fit like a glove—like a glove," she repeats. "I don't feel any of the issues I feel when I am at home. Except I don't eat the fried tarantulas or the grasshoppers. I bring my peanut-butter-and-rice-cake sandwich every day."

I don't think I have ever heard Jessica so alive, so animated. She feels part of something. Even though she is a visitor and speaks a different language, she feels that in Cambodia with these girls, she truly belongs.

"Every day I have contact with everyone, all the staff and even my tuk tuk driver, who drives me to and from the shelter every day. Why?" She answers her own question, "Because they all want me to teach them English. I have to give my driver a ten-minute English lesson before we leave the driveway each morning."

Jessica is teaching two classes of English every day. A cat and its three kittens live in the classroom. When class begins, all

230 I BAFFLED BY LOVE

the girls put their hands together, bow and say, "Good morning, teacher." At the end of the class, they bow again and say, "Thank you for teaching us."

"They have learned to rely on each other," Jessica tells me. "In Cambodia, there is no public affection allowed, but here they are so tender. When a girl feels upset or doesn't feel well, one of the other girls massages her head and another hugs her. Hugs and physical contact are great salves for these girls. They hug me, too. The three-year-old bows when he sees me, and then he jumps into my arms."

I think to myself, *How very healing safe touch must be.*

"The nights are hard sometimes," Jessica continues. "I feel sad; I remember things from when I was young. The adults in my life didn't treat me right. They were supposed to be loving and nurturing, and they weren't. All the affection with the girls is really nice, but it is painful, too, you know, because it reminds me of what I did not have."

Jessica is so articulate about what is stirred for her; it is truth, her truth, and she can share it with me, with others and, most importantly, with herself.

"It is remarkable how easily you are able to give and receive affection now," I tell her.

"True," she acknowledges. "Oh, Laurie, it is time for us to say good-bye." She pauses. "You know, I don't think I could be doing this if I didn't have this time on Skype with you, and with Harry in the mornings."

———

Jessica and I continue to Skype once a week. She is able to be present with the girls at the shelter and recognize her own feelings. The dissociation, the flatness of her feelings, has shifted. She struggles at night, but she does not falter. She uses her skills to calm and to soothe herself.

The girls teach her how to style her hair. Several of them are studying to be hairdressers. She teaches them English and more.

Today when we Skype, Jessica tells me about Mora. "Mora speaks pretty good English. I see her first thing in the morning. She says when she wakes up, she feels really tired. She dreams all night about her mother and her father, who is not a nice guy. I have experienced this waking state of exhaustion many times. Then Mora asks me how she can make her dreams stop, and I think, *What would Laurie say?* I felt myself saying things like you would say. I told her that the people in her dreams might also be parts of herself. We talked for a while. I told her I was glad she could talk to me about her dreams, about the things she worries about. I told her about you and Harry and that it makes a difference to have someone you trust to talk to. Mora hugged me and said, 'You made me feel better.' Then this other girl comes along, and now she is hugging me, and then she puts her head in my arms. She is getting comfort from me. It is like that all day. It makes me feel so good."

"You are such a gift to those girls," I say.

"I learned it from you," she replies.

"Maybe you learned the skills, but it takes courage, too. And that is all yours."

"I feel like my brain is growing," she says. "I used to feel so separate from myself; now my feelings and my thoughts come through all of my pores. I am more me, and I like that."

It is time for us to say good-bye. We gaze at each other. Jessica puts her hands together and bows and says, "Thank you, teacher."

Chapter 37: I LOVE YOU, TOO

"**M**ama!" The baby reaches for her mother. They are one. Their bodies connect: breast to mouth, eyes gazing at each other. Her milk is comfort and sustenance, and it quiets the hungry child. They are falling in love. Soon the mother cannot imagine life without the child, and the child does not know life except through her. The mother will love, nurture, cherish, and protect the child. This is as it should be. She is fierce, protective of this life she has created. Their bond is the foundation for all the child's future relationships.

The mother's attunement to her child's needs, moods, and desires allows the child and, later, the adolescent, to thrive; the child's brain becomes hardwired for love, a map and compass for life's journey. Healthy, safe attachments feed the soul, they give birth to the capacities for empathy and reflection that are necessary for love. These bonds also provide the child with comfort when something frightening happens. Within the cradle of this secure attachment, the child learns to find and benefit from the comfort of another; later, she will find her own rhythms and will learn to comfort herself, a skill we call resilience.

For many of my clients, the people who were supposed to provide this emotional sanctuary were unpredictable or absent.

My clients did not bask in the loving gaze of another; they were not soothed when they were scared. They weren't given the early sense of safety that is required in love. You cannot honestly love someone you fear.

Some people say it is most important that we love ourselves, but love is not a solo performance; it requires the resonance of another. If you have not known love, loving yourself is impossible.

It is well accepted that the therapeutic relationship must provide clients with the experience of a secure attachment. This is foundational for facilitating healing. Therapists must be predictable, maintain good boundaries, and offer empathic responses. In this context, therapy can provide a corrective emotional experience. But this doesn't suffice to repair the injuries caused by the chronic absence of love, and emotional and physical safety. For that, more is required.

Love is the opposite of abuse; it goes beyond what is required for a secure attachment. It entails a passionate commitment to the other's well-being, and accountability for mistakes and omissions. It is visceral, revealing itself in expressions of pride in another's successes, or in tears at another's pain.

Love is expressed in a constellation of words, feelings, and actions that nourishes vitality, gives life meaning and fosters resilience.

I want my clients to know they can walk away from people who do not value them, and toward those who will love them well. I want abuse to be unacceptable in their relationships. I want them to recognize mutuality and to understand who is worthy of their trust. I want them to have the capacity to love.

The secret of my profession is that many therapists *do* love their clients, though this is seldom acknowledged. I was taught to treat these feeling of love with suspicion, to guard them carefully for fear they could do harm. Nobody ever cautioned me that the withholding of these feelings of love could also do damage.

Love, I have come to understand, is not indulgent; it is unkind to require too little in love.

When a child's love is not received with pleasure, the child is crushed. The most precious thing all of us have to offer another human being is our love. When I have been unable to receive my client's expression of love with pleasure, I have done them a great disservice.

What I now understand, but did not understand when Martha, my blunt client, demanded to know if it would kill me to tell her I love her, too, is that therapy is, at its best, a love story. It is a story about the repair of love—the restoration of the capacity to love and be loved. I have come to believe that learning about love, for many survivors of childhood abuse, is the subtext of our work together.

Today, when Martha gets up to leave, her hair tucked under her Yankees cap, she turns to me and says, "I love you."

I smile warmly and say, "I love you, too."

There are also other clients to whom I can now say, "I love you." I do not say these words often, but neither do I say them infrequently.

I remember the first time my daughter tasted ice cream. Her entire body was startled with the delight of this new discovery, with this new possibility of pleasure. So, too, for many of my clients, the good kind of love—love paired with integrity, commitment, and tenderness; love that embraces a keen devotion to their well-being—was unimaginable. Many have never heard the words "I love you" spoken to them. Others have, but they were accompanied by actions that contradicted them.

When I break the convention of my profession, when I dare to utter the words, "I love you," love can be known, recognized. For some of my clients, this is their first experience of love that is supportive, healing, and genuine.

Love, like ice cream, is messy at times, but who would want to live in a world without it?

Chapter 38: MY MOTHER LEARNS TO PRAY

Daisies, yellow roses, and purple lilacs adorn the mantle of my fireplace. This is definitely my mother's influence. She taught me that a house filled with flowers delights the eye and enlivens the spirit. Because of her, I can also shop with an eye for a unique style, unafraid to spend an occasionally unreasonable amount of my paycheck on the jacket or sweater that ties the whole outfit together.

I have come to have very tender feelings toward my mother. We laugh together and walk the streets of Manhattan, shopping, browsing, and noticing all the vendors' wares on New York's sidewalks. She knows all the vendors with the better goods and the best deals. My mother has come to feel more like home to me.

When she began to show signs of aging, my mother wanted and needed more of my care and attention. Initially, I resented this. *Where was she*, I thought, *when I was in need, small and unable to fend for myself?* But those feelings, though powerful, have passed. We have entered a new chapter in our lives.

My mother acknowledges how little she knew about love when she was younger. She says she has learned more about love, about loving, from me and from others. She regrets her failures, her self-centeredness. My mother is now in her mid-nineties, and I have fallen in love with her.

Betsy gets pleasure from simply hearing my voice. She lights up when we speak on the phone or she sees my face. I have become someone special—central, actually—in my mother's life. My daily call to her is a new part of my everyday ritual, like texting my grown children or kissing my husband good-bye in the morning. Now there is the, "Hi darling," "Hi, Mom" ritual. I like it. How strange this coming together is, this tender moment we both have come to cherish.

Betsy tells me how she hates walking with a cane on the uneven sidewalks of the Upper East Side. Though she has outlived most of her friends, and my father by fifteen years, she resents the cruelty of aging, its assaults on her body. Her balance is shaky; she hates that she is no longer the golfer who could hit a ball farther than most men. She also dislikes that the theater, even movies, are less enjoyable now that her loss of hearing erases the nuance of dialogue. Her sources of pleasure are shrinking.

Still, she walks with her cane to the high-end grocery on Third Avenue across the street from her apartment, with its fresh flowers protected under the red awning, and picks up a bouquet for her bedroom (and another for the den, if company is expected). This is also where she goes to get her dinner: a grilled chicken breast with goat cheese, marinated peppers and arugula on a roll, or a simple grilled baby lamb chop with mint pesto.

This is my mother's 'hood, the world of fresh flowers and mint pesto.

I visit more often. We navigate the New York sidewalks together, walking arm in arm. She holds on to me so I can steady her. We pass my favorite clothing shop, and she encourages me to go in. She finds a chair and places her cane next to her. I try on an oversized, flowing black top. I come out of the dressing room to find her across the room on the comfy upholstered chair. She looks me over, squeezes her face like she has eaten a sour lemon, and shakes her head no. I believe her.

We chat as we walk the streets that circle her home. Betsy says what she has said to me before, that she is unsure if she ever really loved anyone. Today this strikes me as rivetingly sad. I know that she loves me and I love her, but we are both crippled in our ability to express love to each other, though we say the words freely.

Our relationship is now warm and caring, but I still notice a subtle resistance inside me that interferes with a freer, unbridled expression of love for my mother. Something feels hardwired in me, difficult to budge.

I wonder if it began before I had words, a primitive imprint on my heart from when my mother was afraid to hold her child, me, in her arms. Or maybe I have not completely forgiven my mother. I wonder if I am holding on to a small strand of disdain for my mother to honor the hurt child of my childhood. For many years, I grieved in therapy with Natalie the many losses of my childhood—losses that came from having a mother who could not give me the love I desperately needed. My relationship with Natalie repaired something. Have I not forgiven my mother as totally as I once believed I had?

I know my mother loved me the best she could, but she still cannot see me. She often says, "Oh, Laurie. You work too hard"—but I do not feel soothed. She does not express pride in my accomplishments or admire the professional craft I have cultivated for many years. She does not acknowledge my successes or admire the ways I have made a difference in the lives of others. She is unaware of what I cherish in life, of the dreams and values that inspire me.

But we have become good friends. Shopping is our shared pastime, how we dance together, how we explore, play, and, yes, spend money. On the streets of New York, in and out of shops, we are mother and daughter. In matters of shopping, fashion, and jewelry, I value her advice and seek her guidance.

Also, when I was a single parent, Betsy was a great companion. We spoke often. She always inquired about the daily events in my daughter's life. She giggled with me when I described my day attending the off-key band performance, Emily's fifth grade debut, when she attempted to get her trumpet to make the appropriate sounds. I still send Betsy paint samples and photos before I change my living room wall colors so she can advise me.

Betsy's strength and stamina are declining. Her cane is replaced with a walker. She hates being a member of this club of old people in New York pushing four-wheeled walkers, though she enjoys its handy compartments for groceries and small packages. Her needs for care are changing rapidly too. I want to make sure she is in good hands. So, during my next visit, I hire Mary. She is all-Irish: warm, loving, and competent. She knows about death and compassion in ways that strike me as far beyond the ordinary. She takes a liking to my mother, and my mother falls in love with her. I love Mary, too. Outsourced love is familiar to both of us.

Mary makes dinner and then tucks my mother in bed before she leaves each night. If she is worried about my mother, she gets one of her Irish friends to spend the night in the apartment. She accompanies her to all her doctor appointments. She takes careful notes, which she shares with me.

———

Betsy calls; her voice is weaker.

"How are you?" I ask.

"Not so good," she says. "But tell me about you."

She has fallen again.

"Promise no hospitals," she says. "I want to die at home."

———

This visit, Betsy wants to talk about death. She wants to go over her will once more and talk about the treasures she will leave behind. She wants to pass things on to her daughters, her descendants. She points to a jade cup on the bookshelf that belonged to her mother. "That was Edna's," she reminds me. "The shelf over the couch is an English antique. Do you or maybe your sister want it? I think the small breakfront is a William and Mary piece; it is worth something. You should sell it when I'm gone. That silver chalice on the coffee table is from Germany. It was your great-grandfather's."

Then there's her mother's mahogany game table and the big corner piece with the vintage leaded glass, the Tiffany clock, and the French provincial chair.

I try to interrupt. I gently place my hand on her shoulder. "I know, Betsy. We have gone over this before."

She is not deterred. "That's a Crown Derby bowl. Maybe it is really worth good money. The light fixture on the desk was Edna's and so were the lamps by the couch."

I am grateful she wants us to have these pieces of her, but I want small things: the lace tablecloths hidden in the bottom drawer, a few of her flower vases, and the small porcelain pitchers we collected together over the years while browsing antique shops.

Legacies, I want to tell her, are not made of antiques or mahogany.

As I prepare to return to Chicago, Betsy becomes alarmed. "Laurie, I didn't finish writing my will."

"Mom, you can tell me your wishes. I will make sure they are honored."

She smiles sweetly and strokes my hand. She is no longer capable of reviewing the will she has gone over dozens of times.

"I want to die in my home," she tells me again. She wants to be surrounded by her antiques, in her cheerful yellow bedroom with the view of Manhattan's cityscape from twenty floors up. This is her home. No hospitals. She makes me promise, and I do.

The hospice workers have taken to calling her Betty. They stop by once a week to check on her. They bring an oxygen tank and place it in the corner of her living room behind the six-foot-tall orange tree. They put morphine in the refrigerator, just in case. My mother requests a spiritual counselor, so they provide that too.

Betsy wants to talk about life. She wonders if there is a God, and wishes she could be a believer. She says she has regrets. Secretly, I hope she will confess her flaws as a mother, but that is not her priority. We talk about her life, but I remind her and myself that I am not her therapist. I am her daughter. I don't want to be her confessor. I want to be kind, to stroke her back and shoulders, to steady her on her walker. I am preoccupied and worried about my mother's well-being. Doing these things for my mother is strangely intimate, more intimate than I have been able to experience before with her.

I was planning to see Betsy next week, for her ninety-fifth birthday, but Mary calls and says I should come now. I call my sister and we book flights.

I am afraid.

"It's the driveway on the left," I tell the cab driver, the direction I have uttered hundreds of times. This time is different. My mother won't remind the doorman that her daughter is arriving. She will not be waiting eagerly by the door when I arrive. She will not remind me to spit out my gum.

I watch my mother in her bed by the window, her face striped with the sunlight entering between the blinds. The soft green-and-yellow wool blanket is pulled up to her breasts. The pink and baby blue strands of embroidery of her nightgown make her look regal, even on her deathbed. Her gold-plated watch is still on her wrist. Her skin is as smooth as a baby's.

As a child, I perfected withholding love from my mother. I did not understand that my mother had wounds that impaired her ability to nurture her children. She, too, felt like a motherless child. Her privileged childhood included a governess, a chauffeur, and even a pony, but none of these eased her unmet longing for a mother's love. As a child, I did not understand how the losses from her past isolated all of us from each other. The misalliances in our family were also beyond my understanding. I wanted to be cherished. I saw delight in my father's eyes, and that was my drug of choice.

When I fired my mother, banning her from my inner life, we both lost so much.

Now, I tenderly stroke my mother's face as she sleeps. Her expression is peaceful, relaxed, inviting. I want to stay close to her; I take her hand in mine. I weep quietly so I do not wake her.

Later, as I walk through the streets, grief inhabits my body. I am shaking with grief. I don't want her to die. I don't want to lose her. I hear a young part of me scream, *I don't want to lose my mother again.*

Early the next morning, Betsy awakens. She announces, "I want to die."

She asks if someone, really anyone, will teach her how to pray.

Then she looks to me and says, "Teach me to pray."

I am sure she does not want me to say the two or three Hebrew prayers I know. She has not fostered a relationship with a God; her Jewish roots are but a fragile thread, and she prefers the bright lights of Christmas trees to the quieter candles of a menorah. I take her hand. I have no idea what I will say next. I hope for some divine guidance.

I say, "I am grateful for all the love around me."

Betsy repeats, "I am grateful for the love around me."

"I believe I am in loving hands."

"I believe I am in loving hands."

"I can be at peace," I say gently.

"What?" she says.

I repeat, "I can be at peace."

My sister adds, "I can surrender to the universe."

Betsy asks her to say that slower.

"I can surrender to the universe," my sister repeats.

My mother knows little about surrender.

For the next several hours, my mother asks that we say these prayers again and again. And we do.

"You are surrounded by love."

One time I add, "I have love in my heart."

"I am in loving hands."

"I can be at peace."

She falls asleep. She looks peaceful. I stay next to her bed. She opens her eyes, half asleep, and looks at me looking at her. She smiles and says, "You are so pretty," and she quickly drifts back into sleep.

Hours later, she awakens in a startle. My sister and I are sitting beside her bed. She looks up at us.

"Laurie, it's not working! I didn't die." She pauses and says, "Did we waste the whole day praying?"

"Mom, it's a process, not a declaration," my sister gently explains.

My mother is not comforted. She is a novice at prayer.

"Mom, you know how we cook a turkey on Thanksgiving?" I say. "Remember, we preheat the oven, prep the turkey, and put it in the oven. Then we baste it, and then we baste it again, and again. It can't be rushed. It has to cook at its own pace."

"Oh," she says. "Maybe tomorrow I can die."

My sister leans toward her and whispers, "Betsy, we are here with you. All that is left is love."

That night I check in on her after dark. I get on her hospital bed and lie next to her. I spoon her. We are close, our bodies touching. I am not withholding, not even a morsel. My feelings of love are spilling from me to her, unguarded, unconditional, and pure.

We both surrender.

Sources and Related Work:

A SELECTIVE BIBLIOGRAPHY

Chefetz, Richard A. *Intensive Psychotherapy for Persistent Dissociative Processes: The Fear of Feeling Real* (Norton Series on Interpersonal Neurobiology). New York: WW Norton & Company, 2015.

Chu, James A. *Rebuilding Shattered Lives: Treating Complex PTSD and Dissociative Disorders.* Hoboken: John Wiley & Sons, 2011.

Cozolino, Louis. *The Neuroscience of Human Relationships: Attachment and the Developing Social Brain* (Norton Series on Interpersonal Neurobiology). New York: WW Norton & Company, 2014.

Dalenberg, Constance J. *Countertransference and the Treatment of Trauma.* Washington, DC: American Psychological Association, 2000.

Freyd, Jennifer J., and Pamela J. Birrell. *Blind to Betrayal: Why We Fool Ourselves We Aren't Being Fooled.* Hoboken: John Wiley & Sons, 2013.

Freyd, Jennifer J. *Betrayal Trauma: The Logic of Forgetting Childhood Abuse.* Cambridge: Harvard University Press, 1998.

Gartner, Richard B. *Betrayed as Boys: Psychodynamic Treatment of Sexually Abused Men.* New York: The Guilford Press, 1999.

Mikel Brown, Lyn, and Carol Gilligan. *Meeting at the Crossroads: Women's Psychology and Girls' Development.* Cambridge: Harvard University Press, 1992.

Gilligan, Carol. *In a Different Voice: Psychological Theory and Women's Development.* Cambridge: Harvard University Press, 1982.

Gilligan, Carol. *The Birth of Pleasure: A New Map of Love.* New York: Random House, 2011.

Gilligan, James. *Violence: Reflections on a National Epidemic.* New York: Vintage Books, 1997.

Gottschall, Jonathan. *The Storytelling Animal: How Stories Make us Human.* New York: Mariner Books, 2012.

Herman, J. L. "Shattered States and their Repair: An Exploration of Trauma and Shame." In The John Bowlby Memorial Lecture presented at the Centenary John Bowlby Memorial Conference, vol. 2007. 1907.

Herman, Judith Lewis. *Trauma and Recovery.* Vol. 551. New York: BasicBooks, 1997.

hooks, bell. *All About Love: New Visions.* New York: William Morrow, 2000.

Jordan, Judith V., ed. *Women's Growth in Diversity: More Writings from the Stone Center.* New York: The Guilford Press, 1997.

Kahn, Laurie. "The Understanding and Treatment of Betrayal Trauma as a Traumatic Experience of Love." *Journal of Trauma Practice* 5, no. 3 (2006): 57-72.

Miller, Jean Baker. *The Healing Connection: How Women Form Relationships in Therapy and in Life.* Boston: Beacon Press, 2015.

Ogden, Pat, Kekuni Minton, and Clare Pain. *Trauma and the Body: A Sensorimotor Approach to Psychotherapy.* New York: WW Norton & Company, 2006.

Pearlman, Laurie Anne, and Karen W. Saakvitne. *Trauma and the Therapist: Countertransference and Vicarious Traumatization in Psychotherapy with Incest Survivors.* New York: WW Norton & Company, 1995.

Perry, Bruce D., and Maia Szalavitz. *Born for Love: Why Empathy is Essential—and Endangered.* New York: HarperCollins, 2010.

Perry, Bruce Duncan, and Maia Szalavitz. *The Boy Who Was Raised as a Dog: And Other Stories from a Child Psychiatrist's Notebook—What Traumatized Children Can Teach Us about Loss, Love, and Healing.* New York: BasicBooks, 2007.

Rogers, Annie G. *The Unsayable: The Hidden Language of Trauma.* New York: Random House, 2006.

Salter, Anna C. *Predators: Pedophiles, Rapists, and Other Sex Offenders: Who They Are, How They Operate, and How We Can Protect Ourselves and Our Children.* New York: BasicBooks, 2004.

Salter, Anna. *Transforming Trauma: A Guide To Understanding And Treating Adult Survivors of Child Sexual Abuse.* Thousand Oaks, CA: Sage Publications, 1995.

Singer, Tania, and Olga M. Klimecki. "Empathy and Compassion." *Current Biology* 24, no. 18 (2014): R875-R878.

Singer, Tania, Ben Seymour, John O'Doherty, Holger Kaube, Raymond J. Dolan, and Chris D. Frith. "Empathy for pain involves the affective but not sensory components of pain." *Science* 303, no. 5661 (2004): 1157-1162.

Solomon, Andrew. *Far from the Tree: Parents, Children, and the Search for Identity.* New York: Scribner, 2012.

Van der Kolk, Bessel A. *The Body Keeps the Score: Brain, Mind, and Body in the Healing of Trauma.* New York: Penguin Books, 2015.

Wallin, David J. *Attachment in Psychotherapy.* New York: The Guilford Press, 2007.

ACKNOWLEDGMENTS

Baffled by Love emerged from thirty years' work as a psychotherapist treating the relational impact of childhood trauma. I want to acknowledge the extraordinary contributions to the field of trauma by Judith Herman, Carol Gilligan, Constance Dalenberg, David Wallin, Bessel Van der Kolk, Allan Schore and Louis Cozolino, and Bruce Perry; their ideas, research, and writing have been foundational in my understanding of trauma and its treatment.

Jennifer Freyd's writing and research on betrayal trauma has deeply affected my practice of psychotherapy, and shapes the narrative of this book. Her steadfast encouragement and friendship has been an unexpected gift.

After many years as a practicing psychotherapist, I went back to school to expand my skills as a writer. I want to thank the faculty at Goucher College's Creative Nonfiction MFA program. I am grateful to Dick Todd, an exquisite teacher and editor, who could imagine a book evolving from my early musings and rough drafts; to Suzannah Lessard, who taught me that the structure of a book is a path to creativity; to Diana George, who believed in her heart that this book could make a difference in others' lives; and to Tom French, a master storyteller.

It was my good fortune to continue to work with Tom French after I graduated. He was my guiding light through the many years and many drafts of *Baffled by Love*.

I could not have endured the years of cycling excitement and doubt without a circle of gifted writers. My thanks to Rita Balzotti, Betsy Armstrong, Jen Cullerton, and Margaret Ghielmetti who contributed companionship, insights, and encouragement.

To my friends Jan Yourist, Jesse Kaufman, Al DeGenova, Don Catherall, Molly Guzzino, Mitch Milner, Esther Lieber, and Emma Kowalenko, who read early drafts: thank you.

My sister-in-law Sharon Bloyd-Peshkin, a professor of journalism at Columbia College, brought patience, kindness, and a keen editing eye to the final rendering of this manuscript.

Treating trauma is difficult and truly impossible without a community of trusted and talented colleagues. Womencare Counseling and Training Center has been my professional home. I have been privileged to know and work with some of the most talented, compassionate clinicians. I want to thank Judith Ierulli, Amy Chandler, Amy Stienhauer, Beth Katz, Ellen Lonnquist, Beth Holzhauer, Monica Robinson, Alissa Catiis, Sara Powers, and Jen Cutilletta for years of collaboration and mutual support.

Janet Migdow, my dear friend, is also my primary professional collaborator. She is the co-creator of the Trauma Consultation Training program in which we have mentored hundreds of trauma therapists, who continue to work on the front lines with trauma survivors who are marginalized and too easily forgotten.

Behind every first book there are angels who blow on your wings until you can fly. My sister, Susan Jill Kahn, offered her insights as an experienced and gifted psychotherapist and read many early drafts, offering endless encouragement. My father-in-law, Murray Peshkin, believed in me and in this book and told me so whenever my confidence would waver.

Thank you to my children Ariana, Danielle, Emily Rose, and Matthew. They are the family I always wanted, in which everyone is cherished and love is never in short supply.

My deepest gratitude is to my husband Michael, whose love and devotion is more than I had imagined was possible. His belief in me and my dreams continues to sustain my spirit.

This book would not be in your hands without the pioneering spirit of Brooke Warner and her vision for She Writes Press.

Most of all, I want to thank my clients, who have allowed me to share their stories and our story, so others could be inspired by their struggle to find new understandings of love. My clients are my best teachers and the inspiration for this book.

ABOUT THE AUTHOR

Laurie Kahn MA, LCPC, MFA a pioneer in the field of trauma treatment, founded Womencare Counseling and Training Center in 1980. Since then, her ideas and expertise have served clients who have experienced childhood abuse, as well as hundreds of clinicians who have graduated from her Trauma Consultation Training Program. Her most salient contribution to the field is the concept of child abuse as specifically a traumatic experience of love.

Kahn's personal essays have been published in anthologies, and her articles and book reviews in professional journals. She lives in Evanston, Illinois with her husband, Michael, and her labradoodle, Kali.

Author photo © Bill Burlingham

SELECTED TITLES FROM SHE WRITES PRESS

She Writes Press is an independent publishing company
founded to serve women writers everywhere.
Visit us at www.shewritespress.com.

Say It Out Loud: Revealing and Healing the Scars of Sexual Abuse by Roberta Dolan. $16.95, 978-1-938314-99-5. An in-depth guide to healing the wounds caused by sexual abuse, written by a survivor who's lived the process firsthand.

Tell Me Your Story: How Therapy Works to Awaken, Heal, and Set You Free by Tuya Pearl. $16.95, 978-1-63152-066-2. With the perspective of both client and healer, this book moves you through the stages of therapy, connecting body, mind, and spirit with inner wisdom to reclaim and enjoy your most authentic life.

Singing with the Sirens: Overcoming the Long-Term Effects of Childhood Sexual Exploitation by Ellyn Bell and Stacey Bell. $16.95, 978-1-63152-936-8. With metaphors of sea creatures and the force of the ocean as a backdrop, this work addresses the problems of sexual abuse and exploitation of young girls, taking the reader on a poetic journey toward finding healing from within.

Letting Go into Perfect Love: Discovering the Extraordinary After Abuse by Gwendolyn M. Plano. $16.95, 978-1-938314-74-2. After staying in an abusive marriage for twenty-five years, Gwen Plano finally broke free—and started down the long road toward healing.

Secrets in Big Sky Country: A Memoir by Mandy Smith. $16.95, 978-1-63152-814-9. A bold and unvarnished memoir about the shattering consequences of familial sexual abuse—and the strength it takes to overcome them.

Not Exactly Love: A Memoir by Betty Hafner. $16.95, 978-1-63152-149-2. At twenty-five Betty Hafner, thought she'd found the man to make her dream of a family and cozy home come true—but after they married, his rages turned the dream into a nightmare, and Betty had to decide: stay with the man she loved, or find a way to leave?